First Printing, 2015
Title: The Beginner Blueprint
Sub-title: From Zero to Hero, Your Road Map to Success, No Matter What Your Goal
Book Series: A Way of Living
Author: Sandra Phillips

ISBN   978-0-9942272-0-1 (paperback)
ISBN   978-0-9942272-2-5 (EPub)

Ordering Information: Quantity sales. Special discounts are available on quantity purchases by corporations, associations, and others. For details, contact the author on the email address below.

Website: www.aWayOfLiving.com.au
Email: sandra@aWayOfLiving.com.au

Edited by: Martin Phillips, Debbiie Strazzari, Janet Payne
Cover Design by: Zizi Iryaspraha Subiyarta / www.pagatana.com

Learn more about the underlying philosophy that has inspired *A Way of Living Book Series.* Please visit www.Karate4Life.com

KARATE 4

THE BEGINNER Blueprint

Contents

Acknowledgements	iv
Preface	v
A Way of Living overview	x

1. A NEW CHALLENGE	1
• It all started with a decision	2
• Committing to a challenge	5
• This challenge is no longer about me	8
• Borrowed confidence	10
✗ Story - Inspirational people: Digging deeper to find your best	14

2. PERSEVERANCE & PATIENCE   19

- The joys of being a beginner   20
- A loving family   24
- Marathon time   28
- ✗ Story - Inspirational people: Making the most of every opportunity   34
- I'm going to Japan   38
- Counting down - One month to go   40
- Counting down - Two weeks to go   43
- Time to race!   46
- ✗ Story - Inspirational people: Staying true to yourself   52

3. REVEALING THE REWARDS   59

- Reflecting on a great journey   60
- Limiting beliefs   63
- Serving others   64
- ✗ Story - Inspirational people: A great student will always attract great opportunities   66

4. THE BEGINNER BLUEPRINT   71

- A thought on the path to achieving your goals   72

THE BEGINNER Blueprint

Contents

Acknowledgements   iv

Preface   v

A Way of Living overview   x

1. A NEW CHALLENGE   1

- It all started with a decision   2

- Committing to a challenge   5

- This challenge is no longer about me   8

- Borrowed confidence   10

Story - Inspirational people: Digging
deeper to find your best   14

2. PERSEVERANCE & PATIENCE   **19**

- The joys of being a beginner   20
- A loving family   24
- Marathon time   28

✗ Story - Inspirational people: Making
the most of every opportunity   34

- I'm going to Japan   38
- Counting down - One month to go   40
- Counting down - Two weeks to go   43
- Time to race!   46

✗ Story - Inspirational people: Staying
true to yourself   52

3. REVEALING THE REWARDS   **59**

- Reflecting on a great journey   60
- Limiting beliefs   63
- Serving others   64

✗ Story- Inspirational people: A great
student will always attract great opportunities 66

4. THE BEGINNER BLUEPRINT   **71**

- A thought on the path to achieving
your goals   72

Story - Inspirational people: A shift in
perspective could be all that is needed   77

· The beginner blueprint overview   82
· Breaking down the beginner blueprint   84
· Leading by example   119

Story - Inspirational people: All
interactions begin and end with respect   121

5. SHARE YOUR STORY   **125**
· Thank you for reading the
beginner blueprint   126
· Everybody has a story   128
· How to submit your story   130

6. ABOUT THE AUTHOR   **131**

Hold onto your dreams

Let go of the details

Act with Love

Acknowledgements

As much as I love a great adventure, I couldn't have completed this adventure without a whole lot of support from my husband Martin and children, Sami and Steven. Thank you!

A special thank you to everyone at the Sunshine Coast Paddle Sports Club. I received some great instruction from Margaret King, Peter Petho and my training partner, Bob Hamblet.

Thank you to all family and landcrew members who were a part of this adventure. It was certainly a very special adventure which I'll remember for a long time.

I've been a keen writer for some time now, and I've had access to many great resources, mentors and supporters that I knew would someday align me with becoming an author. Up until now though, I knew within my heart it wasn't my time.

There was so much 'force' and 'frustration' surrounding this area of my life, not to mention a lack of self-confidence. The fears and insecurities were heavy and many and kept me tied down with what felt like a ball and chain for many years.

There was a lack of belief in my abilities to write and communicate effectively. I also realised that I would need to pull together a team of experts that could help me and this opened up another can of worms as I analysed my ability as a leader.

I had a realisation a while back about the magnificence of nature. If you ever take the time to observe nature in action, you may also come to realise the absence of elements such as force and frustration.

There is an effortlessness about nature; it is peaceful, harmonious, always changing from season to season and everything happens in the perfect timing. This is the foundation and essence that I wanted to achieve with all my published writings.

The idea of publishing books came to the forefront

of my mind once again just last week. And, right on schedule, that devastating fear came knocking on my door. I have to be honest; physically I felt like I was wiped out, depleted of all life and finding it difficult to keep a calmness about myself. Thankfully I could hold myself together for the majority of the time, yet it wasn't one of my finest weeks as a wife.

It was as if there was a battle going on within me that drained my energy so much that I could have just slept for a whole week. By the end of the week, I was pretty weary but I knew it was time to pull out the book writing resources and go for it.

Now, only four days later, I have expanded my team and we are shaping up to do our first print run of 'The Beginner Blueprint' in just under two weeks.

I am extremely grateful for all the experiences leading up to this moment of putting the finishing touches on 'The Beginner Blueprint'. This will be the first book in the 'A Way of Living Book Series'.

The time is right, my purpose is now far greater than fear. I feel as though I have matured and developed to a point of feeling ready and equipped to tackle the goal of becoming an author.

I smile as I write this as I know I'll make mistakes on this journey. A lot of mistakes. But with continual time and effort, I'll get better. With a touch of luck, I may be able to make a difference in the lives of others.

I would like to thank all of the incredible people that I get to work with every day. As you read The Beginner Blueprint, I will introduce you to a few of these people. I believe all of these people demonstrate qualities required to succeed in our rapidly changing world.

I haven't used real names within The Beginner Blueprint. The people I have chosen know who they are, and I must once again thank them for being in my life. I hope that you will be inspired by these people, celebrate them and know that you too have many great qualities within you.

In case you are asking, why 'Zero to Hero'? That was my husband's idea so you'll have to take it up with him. I certainly don't see myself as being a hero but it is nice to think that maybe I'm a hero in my husband's eyes.

A huge thank you to Martin, Sami and Steven for simply being themselves and allowing me to be myself. As simple as it sounds, it is the most perfect gift to receive from those closest to you. The gift of acceptance and unconditional love.

And, why The *'Beginner'* Blueprint. It was a very deliberate decision on my part to choose the word 'Beginner'. In my mind, it is important to always remain a student of life in all that we do and avoid coming to the conclusion that we know everything.

Often we may know something in theory, but whether or not we are truly applying it to our lives is something very different. When we dare to look a little deeper, we will always find a way in which we can apply ourselves more efficiently and effectively.

The person that chooses to remain a student will continue to dig deeper. They will realise that there is always another level of refinement, which will in turn result in a greater quality of life.

Learning is a never-ending process with great rewards. It has a remarkable compounding effect if we choose to continually and consistently invest time and effort into always being a student of life.

I hope that this book inspires you to learn more about you, your gifts and how you can make a difference in this world.

More Importantly, I hope that you are able to plant the seeds of your dreams in your heart. Nurture them generously with positive thought and learn the value of patience. When the time is right for you, I hope that you will be guided to dig deeper and share your many gifts with others.

If you know that the timing is right for a certain experience in your life right now, then The Beginner Blueprint will help you greatly in your endeavours. It is a simple, yet effective blueprint.

You will stack the odds in your favour to succeed no matter what your goal. The greater the attention to detail, the more enjoyable the experience and greater the result.

I wish you well on your many chosen adventures ahead of you. I trust that you will receive all that you require in terms of time, energy, personal growth, resources and people to help you succeed.

Sandra Philips

A Way of Living Overview

Before I introduce you to The Beginner Blueprint, I wanted to give you the opportunity to become a little more familiar with some of the 'A Way of Living' strategies and perspectives that I have come to adopt in my life.

These ideas have not come about over night, they have been years in the making. Years of trial and error driven by the desire to attract greater happiness without the struggle that once dominated my life.

You can learn more about my story in my 'Design Your Life And Enjoy Purposeful Living Guide'. Within this guide, I walk you through a series of steps to eventually create a plan for your life which will deeply resonate with your heart. This plan will increase your life and help you enjoy greater clarity, creativity, calmness, confidence and contribution in your life.

It is highly recommended to work through the 'Design Your Life And Enjoy Purposeful Living Guide' before tackling The Beginner Blueprint. This process will help you re-unite with the most amazing person that you will ever meet. The one person that can make the greatest difference in your life. You.

Taking time to learn about you, and choosing to deliberately grow yourself from the inside out (develop your foundations), will gift you with greater stability in your life. This stability equates to greater confidence and in time will lead you to setting your sights on more challenging goals. Goals that may have once felt impossible.

This is where The Beginner Blueprint will really come to life and accelerate you towards achieving your goals. When your foundations are continually being refined and strengthened, you have a greater capacity to build the life of your dreams.

In 'Design Your Life And Enjoy Purposeful Living', I share moments in my life where the last thing I wanted to do was to take a look in the mirror. It was always easy to identify weaknesses in others, but it was an extremely uncomfortable and confronting experience to reveal the truth about myself.

So, in my early years, I would go on forcing my way to achieving my goals and give no thought to learning about myself. These were years of struggle and frustration. Years loaded with negative self talk that would eat away any goodness or joy that may have existed in my life.

In taking the time to share a few of my favourite and most effective 'A Way of Living' strategies, it is my hope that you will consider travelling the path less travelled. A path that will:
- Provide you with the foundations to support your greatest dreams.
- Lead you to a way of living without force or frustration.

- Help you find peace, even in the hardest of times.

When you combine these 'A Way of Living' strategies with The Beginner Blueprint, I know that you will be equipped to welcome miracles into your life.

*You Can embrace all weather and all seasons **graciously.***
*You Can **manage your attention** in the moment with each breath.*
*You Can **remain calm and content** with your maturing **perspective.***

*You Can **go with the flow** and **remain flexible** with all challenges.*
*You Can **connect** with yourself and others **always with love.***
*You Can **smile and congratulate yourself** with every mistake.*

*You Can allow yourself to be **filled with confidence and courage.***
*You Can **commit to giving yourself** the attention you need to progress.*
*You Can **be different** (be you) so that **you can make a difference.***
You Can do a lot of little things in your day.

It is my hope that you will soon come to realise that all the little things that you do will all come together and ***make a BIG difference*** in your life and in the lives of others.

A Way of Living Basics

100% RESPONSIBLE FOR YOU
If you want a different result it starts with you. The magic is in your actions and how you spend your time.

ONLY COMPARE YOURSELF TO 'YOU'
If you want to enjoy a powerful, positive & productive state avoid comparing yourself to others. Remove judgement (yourself included) and just enjoy being in the moment.

GIFT OF LIFE
Everyone is special, unique and of value. Choose to learn more about you (self discovery). What do you enjoy? What are you good at?

LIFE IS SEASONAL
It is natural to experience highs and lows in life. What is important is how you respond (thoughts, words and actions).

1. Spring
Plant seeds, choose goals and experiences

2. Summer
Invest consistent time and effort.

3. Autumn
Reap rewards for your efforts.

4. Winter
Reflect. Clear mind and prepare self for new focus.

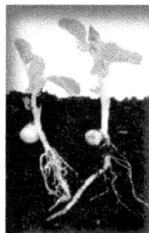

MUSCLES FOR LIFE
'Exercise' these muscles daily to give you the best chance of living the life of your dreams. Take the time to consider adding other qualities to the list below which would help you in your life.

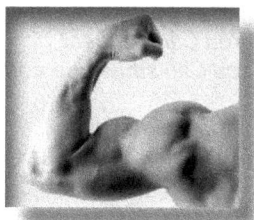

Consistent effort, self discipline, perseverance, patience, focus, a never give up attitude, commitment, respect, trust, gratitude, peace, never rush, never force, do your best, help others, imagination.

LIFE BASICS
Fuel yourself well. Give yourself every chance to be at your best every day so that you can give your best in all that you do.

The Magic Is In Your Actions

PRIORITISE YOUR TIME WITH THE 'TIME PYRAMID'

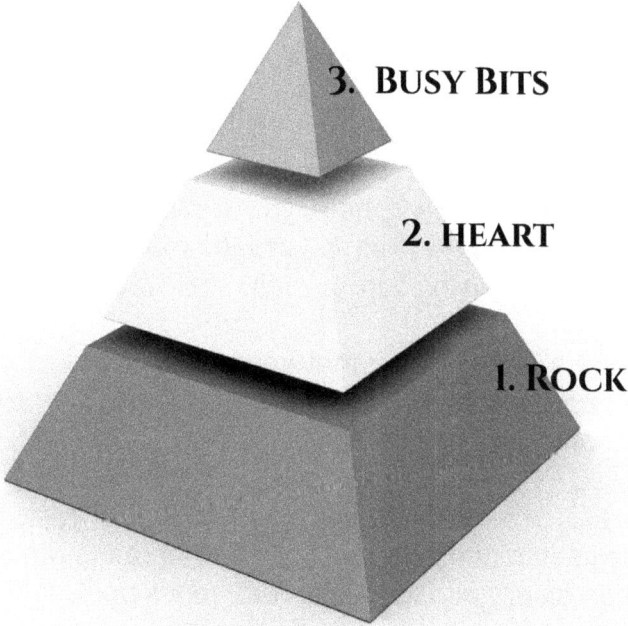

3. BUSY BITS

2. HEART

1. ROCK

The 'time pyramid' is a simple yet very effective tool to help manage your time whilst keeping you aligned with your deepest desires of your heart. We all have 24 hours in a day and it is up to us to choose how we are going to 'spend' (invest) our time.

You'll notice there are three key sections of the time pyramid. When using this time pyramid, the ultimate goal is to spend the majority of your time in section 1 (rock) and section 2 (heart). These two sections make up the very foundations of your life.

Strengthen the foundations of your life and you can build the life of your dreams.

1. ROCK

These are all the things that fuel you in a positive way which will help you be at your best. It is these things that I would make my priority when drawing up a daily or weekly planner.

These are the things that keep me grounded, positive, productive and enable me to help others to the best of my ability.

My top nine fuel sources which I like to track from time to time and see how I can further refine are food, water, sleep, air, self care, rest, movement, sun and family and relationships. Three other important fuel sources that help me be at my best are learning, creating and contributing.

2. HEART

This is where you align yourself with what is in your heart. In my 'Design Your Life And Enjoy Purposeful Living Guide', I take you through a process to identify what is most important to you.

In short, if today was your last day, what would you want your life to be about (your life story)? What would you want to be remembered for?

Each day or week (whatever works best for you), aim to take actions which will deliberately move you closer to living a life based on your life story. This is a life that will resonate with your heart and result in you living a life of satisfaction and significance.

3. BUSY BITS

These are the things that keep us busy, busy, busy. For me it includes things like cleaning (too much), organising others, doing things repeatedly unnecessarily and allowing myself to be distracted with things that can wait.

You could do a mountain of these busy bits in your day and not feel as though you have achieved anything. For me personally, I have found that it is these things that have caused the majority of my stress in the past.

In earlier years, my time pyramid was upside down. I was so busy being distracted by 'busy bits' tasks and activities that I neglected other areas. I eventually started to develop section 1 (rock) of my time pyramid with some great results, but I still wasn't feeling fulfilled.

Years later, I stumbled across section 2 (heart). When I finally understood this element in my life, it was as if

I traded in the stairs for an elevator. The combination of section 1 and 2 as my priority each day, has been one of the most life changing A Way of Living strategies I have ever applied.

You can learn more about the time pyramid within the 'Design Your Life And Enjoy Purposeful Living Guide'.

Results

- There is no failure, simply results of your exploration. Know that your experiences are 'perfect' for you and you are where you need to be, even if it isn't exactly what you wanted. If you don't like your results… remember that change will always start with you.

- Choose to be guided by your heart as opposed to being guided by your mind. Being guided by your mind can often lead us to giving most of our time to the 'Busy Bits' section of the time pyramid.

- For us to achieve our bigger goals we need to give ourselves time to grow into our new and improved selves. Our 'muscles for life' need to be exercised regularly and strengthened. The more growth in our 'muscles for life', the more you will be promoted to higher levels of living in all areas of your life. Be patient.

- No matter what, always focus on doing your best. Keep turning up and do your best.

- As you get better with prioritising your time, you may find yourself moving towards 'managing your attention' to more effectively produce even greater results.

- No matter what happens, always remember that life is much sweeter when you can see the world through the eyes of a child. Have fun, smile and laugh often.

Onwards and Upwards

- You will be challenged and you may question what you are doing. You may also find yourself enduring some tough times where things seem as though they will never work out. Remember, life is seasonal. All will be good with time and continual movement (action). Even on your hardest days, strive to do something which will increase you.

- Be sure to renew your commitment to yourself as you feel the need to re-focus.

- Every day that you adopt the 'A Way of Living' per-spective, you will be putting power into your life. The greater the effort, the greater the reward. The greater your ability to prioritise and manage your time will also enhance your results.

- As a result of exercising your 'muscles for life', (see page xiii) you will grow your confidence and quality of life. The more you strengthen your 'muscles for life', the more comfortable you'll feel to set your sights on bigger goals. Goals that you may have once thought impossible.

- If you find yourself at a sticky point and not feeling progress, it's wise to ask for help. Ultimately you want to keep moving forward. It doesn't matter how fast you move forward but forward is forward. For as long as you keep moving forward you'll be able to experience a favourable change in your circumstances.

If you would like to learn more about the 'A Way of Living' strategies and perspectives shared in this section, please review the 'Design Your Life And Enjoy Purposeful Living Guide.'

Assuming that the foundations of your life are strong, let's get straight into The Beginner Blueprint. Throughout this book, I'll give you a brief recount of a 111km overnight paddling adventure (including preparations for the event). This particular adventure took place on the beautiful Hawkesbury River situated in NSW, Australia.

I had never paddled a day in my life before this paddling adventure. I had only twelve months to prepare, including learning how to paddle. I had absolutely no idea what I was doing and also had to deal with some personal fears.

Fortunately for me, I was able to borrow a touch of confidence from my years of karate training. Not only did my karate experience help me complete this challenge, but it also equipped me with the knowledge and experience to create 'The Beginner Blueprint'. A proven path that can help you achieve your goals.

The very foundations of The Beginner Blueprint have repeatedly helped me secure podium finishes at the International Chito-Ryu Karate-Do Championships many times over for nearly two decades and now it is in your very hands.

In The Beginner Blueprint, I'll introduce a number of everyday people of various ages, all of whom I believe demonstrate qualities required to succeed in our rapidly changing world.

Allow yourself to be amazed by these people, celebrate them and know that you too have many great qualities. By choosing to implement The Beginner Blueprint into your life, you too will achieve your goals in your time and in your way.

I have deliberately designed this book so that you can read it quickly. You can capture the essence of The Beginner Blueprint, and spend the majority of your valuable time working it into your life.

Chapter 1

A NEW CHALLENGE

- It All Started With A Decision
- Committing To A Challenge
- This Challenge Is No Longer About Me
- Borrowed Confidence
- *Story* - Inspirational People: Digging Deeper To Find Your Best

It All Started With A Decision

When you choose to commit to learning something new, you may experience the famous 'honeymoon phase'. No obstacle is too grand in the 'honeymoon phase', and nothing will keep you from achieving your goals.

The goal is fresh and you are feeling motivated. You go charging off the start line with every ounce of energy that you can muster. Often we do this without a plan, equipped only with the heart and courage of a lion.

It is common that many of us, at some point in our lives, will experience giving up on our goals soon after the 'honeymoon phase' is over. Especially if we hadn't previously established a plan and some ground rules for achieving our goal. This is where The Beginner Blueprint will serve you well.

It takes a special kind of person to continue beyond the 'honeymoon phase' and tackle what I call 'facing the giants of the jungle' phase. If you have a plan, you can more easily maintain your focus and purpose whilst navigating yourself throughout the above mentioned phases.

In my experience, actions seem to hold a wealth of power when it comes to influencing and inspiring others to bring forward their best versions of themselves.

This is why I have decided to share one of my recent life changing adventures of participating in an overnight 111km paddle.

"Every accomplishment starts with the decision to try."
~ Unknown

It is my hope that in sharing this adventure, along with The Beginner Blueprint, that you may have another way in which you may move forward to achieve your goals.

Within the following pages, I will share a brief look at a paddling challenge that I welcomed into my life. For me to complete this journey, I had to go back to being a beginner. I had to start from scratch, just as any other person would have to if they decided to start a new hobby or adventure in life.

Fortunately, I was able to borrow a little confidence from my years of karate training. In the end, it all came down to my ability to be a student, trust the guidance of the experts and simply get on the water and put the runs on the board.

Whether you are beginning a new adventure from scratch, or you are at the stage of refocusing and recommitting to a more long term goal, The Beginner Blueprint can work for you.

You can even test The Beginner Blueprint out on things like organising your next family holiday. Choos-

ing simple goals as a starting point is a great way to get a feel for how The Beginner Blueprint works. Then you can step up into more challenging goals.

It all starts with a decision. A decision to welcome an experience or adventure into your life. The decision I made was to participate in a 111km overnight paddle.

Do you have any experiences or adventures that you would like to enjoy in the near future? Take this opportunity to not only read The Beginner Blueprint, but to also piece together a plan for one of your next adventures (big or small).

By the time you get to the end of The Beginner Blueprint, you'll already be on your way to achieving your next goal.

Committing To A Challenge

Choosing to commit to a challenge on water ter-rified me, so I knew that it was the right type of challenge for me on a personal level. I was going to be stretched and expanded in every way possible.

"Commitment is that turning point in your life when you seize the moment and convert it into an opportunity to alter your destiny."
~ Denis Waitley."

Committing to a 111km overnight paddle was pure madness, yet I was looking for a challenge that was going to throw me completely out of my comfort zone. It was a sink or swim challenge, as I would soon find out on my first kayak lesson.

I committed myself to this adventure before I really knew what I was getting myself into. It was only after I took my first paddling lesson that I realised I may have over committed myself. I was not even remotely equipped to handle this challenge and I had less than twelve months to get ready.

At the time of committing to this challenge, I had no prior paddling experience and was by no means a strong swimmer or even a fan of water. I have enjoyed over twenty years of karate training in a dojo which is a relatively friendly environment when compared to the learning environment of a beginner paddler.

As beautiful as the waterways are on the Sunshine Coast, there are so many elements which were out of my control. It was unpredictable and there wasn't a whole lot of room for error.

Despite my lack of experience as a paddler, I was fortunate to be in a position to borrow a touch of confidence from my years of karate training.

Here is the big question. Would all of the knowledge, experience and wisdom acquired over more than twenty years of karate training hold up and get me across the finish line of the 2014 Hawkesbury Canoe Classic?

If you are developing a plan for one of your goals as you read through The Beginner Blueprint, see if you can now develop an awareness of your starting position.

On the next page, you can see the first few steps of the goal setting process outlined in The Beginner Blueprint. My answers are quite brief and are included to give you an example. I give further examples in Chapter 4.

As you work through these sections, be sure to add as much detail as you feel you need to help you achieve your goal.

GOAL SETTING BASICS

1. CHOOSE A GOAL (INCLUDING TARGET DATE)

Example: 111km overnight paddling adventure, taking place on Saturday 25th and Sunday 26th October 2014.

2. MAKE A COMMITMENT (ACTION)

Example: I enrolled in paddling lessons at my local kayaking club.

3. AWARENESS OF YOUR STARTING POINT

Example: I had no prior paddling experience, wasn't a strong swimmer and not a fan of the water. No equipment. Access to local kayak club with experienced coaches and paddlers.

I have been involved in competitive events in karate. This would help me with planning and preparations.

Karate experience would also give me a foundation to build on in terms of mental and physical strength.

This Challenge Is No Longer About ME

On one hand, I had an extremely confronting challenge awaiting me. On the other hand, I had a desire to serve others. This specific challenge was primarily focused on supporting my father-in-law, Roy, who was also doing the race.

"The best way to find your-self is to lose yourself in the service of others."
~ Mahatma Gandhi

When I focused my thoughts on 'the confronting challenge' and associated personal challenges, I was filled with fear. When I focused my thoughts on serving others, in particular Roy, I was filled with excitement.

Although the challenge before me had not changed, I was able to shift my energy from a fearful and non-productive state to a more enthusiastic and productive state. Once again I am reminded of the power of perspective.

Altering my perspective to a more positive and favourable state to complete this challenge was a powerful realisation which was welcomed so early on in this adventure. From time to time I felt my focus turn inwards and I felt defeated before I even really got started.

Thankfully when I looked back at my karate journey, I knew with all my heart that if I could stay focused on the service of others: I could give myself the best chance of turning my thoughts and desires into positive words and positive actions.

Let's now take a closer look at why you want to achieve your goal. Reasons why it is important for you, and reasons why it may help others. Further examples and guidance for this section can be found in Chapter 4.

GOAL SETTING BASICS

4. IN ACHIEVING YOUR GOAL, HOW WILL IT HELP YOU? HOW WILL IT HELP OTHERS?

Example:
Self - Confronting fears, pushing me out of my comfort zone, enjoying nature.
Others - Helping Roy complete 111km race, more time with family.

Borrowed Confidence

In order to establish a plan so I could start preparing for the 2014 Hawkesbury Canoe Classic, I needed to first assess the resources and assets that I had on hand. I had nothing along the lines of equipment, but I did have a collection of experiences and tools with regards to planning and preparing for competitive events in relation to karate.

Fortunately, I had been able to test and measure a great deal in my time both as a competitor and a coach. I have not only become a world champion myself, but I have also coached others to international podium finishes, including numerous world champions.

"You don't have to be great to start, but you have to start to be great." ~ Zig Ziglar

After two decades of testing and measuring within competitive environments, I have pulled together a few key elements which help me be at my best on competition day.

I hope that the following key elements help you with creating a plan to achieve your goals. I won't go into too much detail with examples here, as I explore these in greater detail in *'Chapter 4, The Beginner Blueprint.'*

CREATE A PLAN

1. ESTABLISH A TIME LINE
Start date through to target date, including any check in dates (short term goals, full dress rehearsals, training intensity adjustments, rest periods etc).

2. LISTEN AND LEARN
Ask the right people the right questions.

3. SELF AWARENESS
You are your greatest asset, so invest time into learning more about you and building the foundations of your life. Achieving your goals, will require more than just physical development. Refer to 'Design Your Life & Enjoy Purposeful Living Guide' for further guidance.

4. FAMILIARITY OF EQUIPMENT/TOOLS
Prior to competition day, be confident and comfortable with any equipment you may need.

5. POSITIVE FUEL
Everything in your life is either fuelling you positively or negatively. You need to choose your fuel sources carefully.

6. FAMILIARITY WITH ENVIRONMENT
Familiarity will allow you to be more relaxed, calm and comfortable.

7. SUPPORT TEAM
Who are the key people who can keep you account-able and support you from the start to the achieve-ment of your goal?

8. PRE-EVENT FULL DRESS REHEARSALS
Within your planning, allow for opportunities to practice under pressure. Identify strengths, weaknesses and further refine your game plan for competition day.

9. IMMERSION
Getting started, gaining momentum or changing habits; consider a period of immersion.

10, MEASURING PROGRESS
Develop ways to measure your progress throughout your preparations. This gives you clarity and greater ability to enhance your performance.

___

Please take the time to briefly look at the above ten key elements in conjunction with your goal. You'll find additional guidance and examples in Chapter 4 to help you with creating your plan.

For now, consider starting a new word document on your computer. List the ten key elements as headings, and start to list a few thoughts that come to mind for each one. This will give you a starting point to create your plan.

It will take time, but hang in there. Your plan will give you greater clarity and the ability to relax and enjoy the journey.

As you continue to move through The Beginner Blueprint, you'll more than likely get a few more ideas to add to your plan. Simply add ideas as they come up.

Your plan will soon start to take shape. Get a little creative with the best way to present your plan. It needs to be formatted in a way that works for you. The formatting of my plans has evolved over time and yours will too.

I've gone from very few words to pages of words and back to few words. My only suggestion is that you be mindful that you are a 'work in progress'. Be flexible and prepared for change.

Depending on your results, you may also need to make some adjustments to your plan. It's all good. Make the adjustments and continue moving forward.

Story: Inspirational People

DIGGING DEEPER TO FIND YOUR BEST

A Special Moment With Sally

In the midst of my Saturday morning private lessons, I was scheduled to work with Sally. Sally entered the dojo with her training journal. She greeted me with one of her gigantic smiles which instantly filled me with great joy. It amazes me how kids can share such authentic smiles, which can take you to the most magical places.

We sat down next to the bundle of highlighters and paper that I had prepared earlier for Sally. Sally loves to write and draw, so whenever I see her booked in for a private lesson, I make sure I have plenty of colourful pens and paper.

To share what it is like working with Sally in a private lesson could only be likened to being on a treasure island. We work together to dig up the sand to reveal the many treasures below the surface.

The learning process is an adventure in itself. With every treasure revealed, we are not only developing our karate technique but we are also deliberately developing ourselves.

We literally bounce off each other for the entire 30 minutes. In our own little world, we try to make sense of our technique and the world that we live in.

At times we find ourselves digging without finding anything other than more sand. In terms of karate, it would feel as though we aren't making a great deal of progress, or change in our abilities to demonstrate more refined technique.

But this doesn't seem to bother us. We just keep on digging with a balance of 'Fun' and 'Focus' until we are presented with a breakthrough. There is an understanding that remains in the back of our minds that, with consistent effort, we will eventually be presented with our desired result.

Then there are times when we hit something in the sand, which calls for more exploration to reveal the treasure. This is when Sally's strength of exploration and pursuing greater understanding takes over.

She understands that although she may be starting to develop good karate basics, there is always room for improvement, no matter how advanced she becomes with her studies.

In the short time I have known Sally, I have

never heard her say, 'I know that already, can we do something else' or 'I'm bored.' Sally has been very open to digging deeper and challenging herself to get more out of her training.

To her credit she has had quite a positive impact on many of us at our karate school. I'm almost certain this extends to her schooling and home environments.

MUSCLES FOR LIFE

Although only 7 years of age, Sally has quite a few qualities that we could all apply in our lives. These qualities we'll refer to as 'muscles for life'. When we regularly exercise these muscles, we give ourselves a greater chance of achieving our goals.

CONSISTENT ATTENDANCE

If we are going to move closer to achieving our goals, we need to turn up and play. We need to consistently invest time into our goals. The amount of time and effort required will vary from goal to goal.

LEARNING IS AN ADVENTURE

Every adventure that we choose can include a balance of fun and focus. When we flow with these two elements, not only can we experience growth within ourselves, but we can also help others experience growth in their lives.

Taking the time to share our adventures with others can open the doors to greater enjoyment. It can also present experiences that you may not have had otherwise. It can also present opportunities that may be valuable to help you achieve your goals.

PRO-ACTIVE LEARNER

In the beginning, it is great to be guided by others who know the way. As you get moving, see if you can identity ways to become a more pro-active learner. Choose to take 100% responsibility for you and your results.

Seek people, experiences and education that will support you on your way to achieving your goals. As much as possible, develop the learning quality of 'digging deeper'. There is always more that we can learn and apply to our lives to create even better results.

Chapter 2

PERSEVERANCE & PATIENCE

- The Joys Of Being A Beginner
- A Loving Family
- Marathon Time
- Story - Inspirational People: Making the Most of Every Opportunity
- I'm Going To Japan
- Counting Down - One Month To Go
- Counting Down - Two Weeks To Go
- Time To Race!
- Story - Inspirational People: Staying True To Yourself

The Joys of Being a Beginner

Before long I found myself standing nervously at my local kayak club. I stood there for only minutes waiting to meet my paddling coach, but it felt like hours.

To my surprise I was greeted by a familiar and smiling face. Our family doctor, Margaret, would become my first paddling coach.

"To succeed in life, you need three things; a wish bone, a back bone and a funny bone."
~ Reba McEntire

My first visit to the kayak club was a great success. I was in and out within minutes and I had confirmed my booking for a trial program. Now, what to do whilst I waited for my first paddling lesson.

From memory I had approximately two weeks to wait before my first paddling lesson. This gave me plenty of time to grow more fearful and anxious with every day.

I spent a lot of time flicking through the pages of my internal book, '101 Excuses.' There had to be a reason worthy of getting me out of this adventure. By the time my first paddling lesson come about, I was feeling fatigued and restless. The time spent flicking through my internal book on '101 Excuses' was taking its toll on my energy levels.

My fears dominated my thoughts and left me in a low energy state and with very little sleep. I came extremely close to ending this adventure before I even started. All because I chose to allow my mind to be filled with a whole lot of negativity.

The only reason why I turned up to my first paddling lesson was because of Roy. I had made a commitment to him and I couldn't let him down.

Although I made a truck load of mistakes, there was a life changing 'victory moment' taking place on the inside of me. My victory moment was realising the power of simply turning up and having a go, despite the presence of fear.

This one action helped me to release a great deal of tension, anxiety and worry. With this release of negative energy, I was able to experience a freedom and a sense of achievement.

Some wise person once said to me that freedom was on the other side of fear. This adventure has enabled me to make sense of these words a little more.

Listed here is a quick look at some of the highlights from my first paddling lessons. I've chosen my top five to share with you.

- Paddling with my paddle upside down.

- Getting into my kayak and falling out the other side almost straight away. I had some serious work to do on my balance.

- Trying to paddle in a straight line. That never happened. I would sooner tell Margaret that there was something wrong with the rudder. Margaret was very polite and had Bob check over my kayak. My kayak was just fine.

- For some reason when I tried to turn I'd fall out. Apparently you aren't meant to lean into the corners.

- I didn't quite get my head around just paddling. I developed my own little routine of paddle, capsize and swim. I think by the end of the first paddling lesson, I had nailed this routine.

By the end of my first paddling lesson, I didn't seem to show all that much progress. I was able to develop my unique paddle, capsize and swim routine. I think it would be fair to say that with practice, I added a little style and elegance to this routine.

Unfortunately, any hope of completing a 111km overnight paddling marathon had disappeared. If I was going to help Roy with this adventure, I had a lot of work to do. It was going to take a lot more time than I initially thought and I already had a relatively full schedule.

After much thought, I decided to give myself a three month immersion. My paddling program would simply be thirty minutes per day for three months. Sometimes I would just go and sit in a kayak on the waters edge. Other times I would treat myself to going for a paddle.

Throughout this period, there was considerable progress. There was an emerging confidence in the paddling environment and I was becoming more comfortable with controlling my kayak. Then, there were days where I would leave the kayak club with my tail between my legs looking like a drowned rat.

When I weighed up my experiences at this time, there were a lot more positives then negatives. My focus was developing and my confidence building. I'd have to make a conscious effort to control my thoughts. If I didn't, I would easily fall victim to a mind full of negativity.

A Loving Family

With only nine months to go before the big race, I was finding it difficult to stay positive. My progress was so incremental that it was easy to feel disheartened. It would be so much easier to call it a day.

As a result of my slow progress, I found myself overwhelmed and quite emotional at times. I found myself playing the blaming game as opposed to taking 100% responsibility for myself and my results.

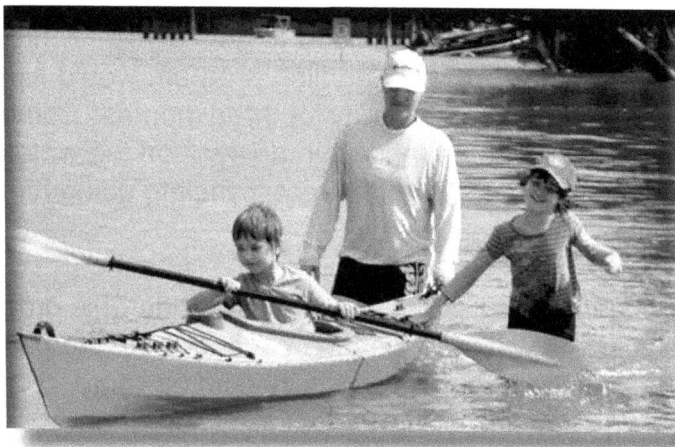

There were times when I would blame Martin. I figured if he had stepped up and did the race with his dad then I wouldn't be in the pickle that I was in. Martin was very patient and continued to support my long hours on the water.

I must admit though, despite my mixed emotions leading up to the big race, I felt so blessed to be experiencing the magnificence of nature. I loved being on the water watching the sun rise. Each morning was different, but they were all stunning.

The more comfortable I grew in this environment, the more I was able to really soak up the beauty of every moment on the water. Even the not so successful days. There was a gift to be found in every experience. I just needed to find it.

I've always had a habit of taking life too seriously, so this was a great adventure to develop my humour a little more. Having the ability to laugh at oneself is a great way to help with the reduction of stress.

Martin was extremely supportive throughout the entire adventure. In the beginning, he was particularly sensitive to the difficulties that I faced. Once I started to relax and loosen up, he found ways to fill my days with more laughter.

> "Coming together is a beginning. Keeping together is progress. Working together is success."
> ~ Henry Ford

I remember one time when Martin and the kids came and watched me paddle. I could hear them laughing from the waters edge. Occasionally, they would shout out words of encouragement at the top of their voices.

I couldn't help but be distracted by the love and joy they shared from afar. It was contagious. Before I knew it, I was smiling and laughing along with them.

I think I spent more time swimming that day, but it was perfect. Martin captured some photos of some of my not so finest moments, whilst I took the opportunity to enjoy the experience and not take life too seriously.

Sami and Steven had a cheeky way about them to keep me from taking life too seriously with this adventure. When I would go paddling, they would ask, "Mum, are you going for another swimming lesson?" They always knew what to say and when.

With the realisation that I wasn't going to quit anytime soon, Martin stepped it up and started collecting equipment. With Martin by my side researching and collecting equipment, I was able to simply focus on paddling.

As it worked out, we ended up investing in an ocean ski. If I was to continue with my usual paddle, capsize and swim routine, I could easily jump back onto the ski wherever I fell off. At least that was the plan assuming that I could master the remount.

Before I got the ski, I would have to drag my kayak back to shore to empty out the water whenever I capsized. That was, if I was lucky enough to be close to shore when I fell out. But that didn't happen all that often.

Generally I was faced with the challenge of dragging the kayak back to some nearby mangroves. I'd have to climb the mangroves like a monkey and somehow empty as much water out as I could before trying to get back in and setting off again.

I must admit, I did get rather creative when I needed to make use of the mangroves. That probably tells you that I visited the mangroves way too many times.

Marathon Time

About 6 months out from the race we ended up with two ocean skis. It was decided that the first ocean ski needed to suit both Martin and myself. A quick adjustment and either of us could have a play. Unfortunately for me, it was quite difficult to transport on my own.

I think I scared Martin one too many times trying to move the ski onto the car on my own. With the length and weight I was destined to drop the ski, damage something in my path or damage myself.

It really became a problem after paddling some of the longer distances, 30km or more. My ability to get the ski off the water, to the clean up area and back onto the car was an accident waiting to happen.

Our second ski was more suited for my smaller frame and it was light. Weighing in at around 10kgs I could transport this ocean ski with ease on my own. Martin could also stay in bed whilst I clocked up the hours on the water.

> "The struggle you're in today is developing the strength you need for tomorrow."
> ~ Unknown

This lighter and more narrow ski is like a rocket and it is more unstable on the water. I had to really work hard on my core strength whilst paddling in this ski, yet I loved the added benefit of how my back would strengthen throughout this adventure.

With the equipment that Martin had collected for me, I was ready to do my first 'full dress rehearsal'. By this time I had been paddling for about six months and I wanted to identify my strengths and weaknesses. I also wanted a point of reference as to how to continue with my preparations.

My goal was to complete 100km over 4 days. I would have Martin and Roy participate for part of this marathon and other times I would be on my own.

Day one of my dress rehearsal marathon, started in the early hours of the morning. Martin, Roy and I headed out for what turned out to be five and a half hours on the water.

We all set off together, but I soon realised that Martin was nowhere to be seen. Roy continued on and I turned back to see if I could find Martin. Martin was still at the boat ramp trying to align his rudder. As soon as we fixed the rudder, we were off again.

Only this time, I was on my own. Roy was a good twenty minutes or more ahead and Martin took off at great pace trying to catch up with his dad.

The further Martin pulled away, the more I started to panic. It was still dark, it was cold and the more I panicked, the harder it was to breathe and keep up. I couldn't believe that my fears came to the surface so early on in this dress rehearsal marathon. I was reduced to tears.

Although I had six months of paddling leading up to this dress rehearsal, I wasn't prepared to deal with the possibility of capsizing in complete darkness.

My mind ran wild with all the craziest 'what ifs' and my heart beat intensified. I tried to call out to Martin for help, but my throat tightened and nothing would come out.

In the distance I could see change in the sky. The sun was rising and replacing the darkness. As I focused on night becoming day, I was able to gain control over my breathing, my vision improved and I could see the waters edge.

A smile come over my face and replaced the tears as I realised that I was paddling so close to the river bank. I wasn't going anywhere fast as I was barely in the river.

Soon I could see Martin. He slowed down at some stage and allowed me to catch up and, before long, we had caught up with Roy. The remainder of paddling on this day was more relaxing and enjoyable.

After five and a half hours on the water, we returned back to the boat ramp. We had completed approximately 28 kms and it was time to take my first step back on land.

Roy and Martin pulled in first and stood up relatively easily. Then, it was my turn. For some reason, I couldn't get out of the ski.

Eventually I got up and I started my slow walk to the car. There was no way I was carrying my ski to the car today, even if it was only 10kgs. I could barely carry myself without stumbling. Thankfully Martin sorted everything out, whilst I made my way to the car. And he did it with the biggest smile which stretched from ear to ear.

My full dress rehearsal marathon continued on despite the state of my body. I was in a lot of pain, but I was determined to complete my four days. With each day, I was becoming more aware of my strengths and weaknesses.

I was able to study the effects of my nutrition, paddling technique, recovery, equipment and, most importantly, how to utilise my mind more effectively.

I didn't get much sleep the night before my final day

of paddling. I spent a great deal of time studying the results that I had collected about my environment, my equipment and myself. The more knowledge I gained the more empowered I was feeling.

I chose to upgrade my game plan to a new and improved version for day four. This one action elevated my confidence and energy levels. It took my focus off the physical pain and directed my attention to creating a game plan that would see me complete day four more efficiently and effectively.

Day four turned out to be the easiest day of my full dress rehearsal marathon. I had learned so much in the first three days that I was able to re-create my game plan to achieve a better result. I was even able to hit a personal best with my average speed.

Participating In a full dress rehearsal at this time was a powerful experience on many levels. The knowledge gained from this experience proved to be invaluable in the lead up to the main event.

"A single feat of daring can alter the whole conception of what is possible."
~ Graham Greene

Story: Inspirational People

MAKING THE MOST OF EVERY OPPORTUNITY

Observing a Genuine Person With a Heart of Gold

Jordan has been in and out of our lives for over ten years now. Watching her grow from afar has been truly inspirational.

In the early years I knew Jordan mostly as a caring parent of three beautiful children. With every conversation and moment that I had with her, I knew there was something special about her.

I wasn't a parent when I first met Jordan, but I just loved her dedication to her family. No matter what she did, she always applied herself with great determination, effort and enthusiasm.

Although she demonstrated such strength of character, it was always wrapped in a gentleness and genuine care for others.

Years later, I am still grateful to have the opportunity to work with Jordan's children at our karate school.

Jordan has also gone on to create a highly successful real estate business whilst balancing her family commitments.

Recently, Jordan set a new challenge, and that was to follow in her children's footsteps and start her own karate program. I am so excited for Jordan, as I know the power of a quality martial arts program.

Jordan will be stretched out of her comfort zone with her martial arts training. However, if she chooses to apply her existing strengths, Jordan will attract a favourable result.

At the time of writing this, Jordan was working through the foundational steps of her karate program with her usual style of determination, effort and enthusiasm.

Jordan's children shared these same qualities of determination, effort and enthusiasm as they edged their way closer to black belt.

I don't know what the future holds for Jordan and her family, but they are certainly stacking the odds in their favour to achieve their goals.

The path to achieving any goal can be long and take a considerable amount of energy. With determination, effort and enthusiasm, I know that you too, will increase your chances of achieving your goals.

MUSCLES FOR LIFE

DETERMINATION

Once you have committed to your goal, consider closing the door behind you.

Once you have closed the back door, you are going to need 'determination' to keep you moving forward. When you commit to new goals, life will find ways to strengthen you.

This strengthening process will enable you to acheive your goals in the perfect time and in the perfect way for you. In the meantime, you'll need to remain determined to continue on no matter what comes your way.

EFFORT

If you have worked hard and applied great effort to achieve previous goals, then you would know the power of effort.

You would have also realised how you can amplify the impact of your effort by being consistent over a period of time.

As you move into managing other people, you'll soon realise the power of the consistent effort of many hands.

One of the hidden bonuses of applying effort to your life, is that of growing your confidence. Next time you are looking at short cutting your way to achieving your goal, remember that you are only hurting yourself.

When you short cut your way to achieving your goals, you aren't strengthening your foundations to welcome even greater success into your life.

ENTHUSIASM

You don't need to be the loudest person in the room to show your enthusiasm, but you do need to be highly interested and engaged in what you are doing.

Aim to combine the works of the mind and body in all that you do. Choose to be a student of life and allow the world to be your playground. There is always more that we can learn.

I'm Going To Japan

With only three months to go, I learned that I was to go to Japan in September. An amazing opportunity to further accelerate my karate studies, yet I would be leaving my family behind for two weeks. My preparations for my 111km paddling adventure would also be interrupted.

"Opportunities are multiplied as they are seized."
~ Sun Tzu

To ensure that I felt ready for training in Japan, I wanted to move my karate training back to the early morning time slot. In doing this, it would align more closely to the training that I would experience whilst in Japan.

With a little bit of creative programming, I was able to pull together a suitable training program. This training program enabled me to continue preparations for both the Hawkesbury Canoe Classic and my Japan trip.

Just before going to Japan I wanted to have one final crack at a marathon paddle. I think it worked out to be about 80kms over two days. I wanted to use this marathon paddle to help me decide which ocean ski I would use at the Hawkesbury Canoe Classic.

Day one, I used our heavier ocean ski. It had greater stability, better storage and it was a very comfortable ride. Day two, I used my lighter and more unstable ocean ski. This is my preferred ski, however the further I paddled, I experienced fatigue and loss of concentration which put me into panic mode.

Yes, I did capsize in my final kilometre. The worst part was trying to get back into my ski. By this time, I was exhausted. It took me a half dozen attempts to get back in and wrap up my practice marathon.

By the end of my 80km paddle, I knew that the heavier ski would be the better choice. My number one priority was safety and comfort and the heavier ski was more suitable. The heavier ski would prove to be a great asset in terms of mental, physical and emotional stability.

One Month To Go

With only three weeks to go until the big race I returned from my training trip in Japan. I was exhausted and feeling the pressure of the big race sneaking up on me. Martin worked miracles with my equipment and clothing, whilst I rested.

Although I rested, I allowed myself to fall victim to a negative mindset. As I returned to good health I felt crippled on the inside and unable to get myself back onto the water to finalise my preparations.

Martin suggested that it was time to go for a paddle. Well, maybe it was more than a suggestion. He packed everything up, drove me to the river and dropped me off.

Within a few minutes of being back on the water, I could feel myself come to life once again. Having three weeks to go was now an exciting thought in my mind.

Sometimes we need a good kick from the people we love. I didn't like being kicked into action and I very rarely need it, but I'm grateful that Martin and his big foot came to the rescue.

At this stage I also stepped up my 'mind fuel' as I was showing signs of self sabotage. This is never fun to endure, but it is very real and you've got to get on top of it or risk having all your hard work come undone.

I seem to be most vulnerable to self sabotage when I'm not actively pursuing my goals. The time away in Japan, followed by a tummy bug, gave me an extended period of time off the water. It was more than enough time to alter my state of mind.

"Rise up and attack the day
with enthusiasm."
~ Unknown

Below are a few examples of how I positively fuel my mind. They are simple, yet highly effective. It was these few strategies that helped me refocus on my adventure.

- Deliberately focus on the good things about this adventure. Personal growth, planning, preparations and contributions from my family and land crew.
- Giving focused energy and thought to all the things I am grateful for in all areas of my life.
- Viewing the world through the eyes of a child. Engaging my imagination and creating positive experiences that give me that 'feel good' feeling about life.

It was about this time as well that I was starting to get eager to have this challenge done and dusted.

With my family's support, I had modified my life considerably to participate in this adventure.

With this in mind, I started to give time and attention to life after this adventure. Prior to wrapping up an adventure, I always like to consider what my next adventure will be moving forward.

Overlapping my goals keeps me from drifting and procrastinating in my life. It keeps me enjoying a life full of adventures and new experiences, whilst embracing the simple things in my life.

Funnily enough, I had a strong pull towards my book writing projects. I didn't do a great deal of planning and preparation at this stage, for my next adventure. It was mostly nurturing the idea with positive thoughts.

I knew that in continually nurturing my goals surrounding book writing with positive thoughts, I would attract the energy, resources and people that I needed to bring this goal to fruition.

My book writing goals have been hanging around in the clouds for quite a few years. I've pulled together the content for four books, but hadn't had the confidence to go to the next step until now.

I trust that all will work out at the perfect time. So whilst I wait I shall continue to develop myself holistically, knowing that all that I learn will equip me with what I need and more, to become a great author of some great books.

Two Weeks to Go

Only two weeks to go and it is time to step it up a notch. What better way to put myself to the test than with another full dress rehearsal. Only this time, I would have all my equipment on board and I would have to endure a longer period of paddling in the dark.

"Forget all the reasons why it won't work and believe the one reason why it will work."
~ Unknown

Bob, my paddling partner, volunteered to come along for the ride and save me if anything was to go wrong. This was my final opportunity to test and measure everything.

This was a relatively short paddle at 25km, as I was starting to feel quietly confident with my preparations. After this final dress rehearsal I would compile all of my results and design a game plan to implement at the 2014 Hawkesbury Canoe Classic.

Here are my top three favourite moments from my final dress rehearsal before the big race.

- I got to wear my ninja beanie and booties. Martin made sure I wasn't going to get cold. Neoprene beanies and booties are very cool.

- I was accompanied by my training partner Bob. Bob has paddled along side of me since starting out on this adventure. He has been instrumental in helping me get set up with the right equipment. He has also shared some great knowledge of the paddling environment.

- Watching the sunrise over the river as we wrapped up our morning paddle. Truly magnificent.

Every adventure has a blooper or two. Thankfully I was becoming more confident and relaxed with this adventure so it was much easier to have a laugh at myself and get on with it. Here are a few bloopers, although there may have been quite a few more.

- I loved my ninja beanie. It was warm and I felt like a bit of a ninja paddling in the dark but as it worked out I couldn't drink my water. Removing the beanie almost meant going for a swim. I'm glad I didn't go for a swim because I had forgotten to attach the GPS correctly to my ski.

- After about 20 minutes of paddling I started to lose feeling in my fingers. I had taped my fingers with coban tape to protect them from blisters. My fingers weren't feeling protected. They were feeling as if they were going to fall off.

- My brilliant food storage idea was a bit of a flop. My food ended up being squashed between my leg and my ski.

As challenges arose I was able to keep a calmness and remain focused on executing my plan. I needed to be flexible and alter my plan from time to time, but all was good now that I had found a flow.

Reflecting on my investment of time and effort up until this point, leaves me feeling a great sense of satisfaction. No matter what happens on race day, I know that I have already won.

I have been able to elevate myself to a place of greater confidence. I have strengthened my 'muscles for life' (refer to viii) and I can sense a growth within myself that has further enhanced my perspective and quality of life.

I love living a life of adventures and experiencing the continual refinement and growth of myself. Most of all, I love helping others experience the feelings associated with living a life of satisfaction and significance, loaded with great adventures.

Time To Race!

Twelve months ago I didn't believe that I would be able to complete a paddling adventure of 111km. Now with only one week to go, I was feeling quietly confident with my preparations and game plan that I had pulled together.

As it worked out, this adventure was loaded with challenges in the final week and during the race. I had a choice to make every time I was greeted with a challenge.

Do you let it get you down or do you just do what you can and keep moving forward? We ended up doing a lot of laughing on this adventure as it seemed to be more appealing than crying and complaining.

The act of planning and preparing assisted greatly in aligning me with a powerful force, that you may know as 'commitment'. When commitment is partnered with 'consistency', an energy starts to brew within you which can be identified as 'confidence'.

With every action throughout your planning and preparation, commitment and consistency work together in harmony to create a whole lot more of this confidence.

Your confidence soon grows to such levels that you find yourself being introduced to another great friend which we'll call 'courage'.

Courage is within all of us and eager to do real work in us, but he'll rarely show his strength and power in our lives unless we first partner up with commitment, consistency and confidence.

Courage was the key ingredient that I needed to get me through the 111km overnight paddle. It was a truly amazing experience, with great people in a magnificent setting.

> "Victory is sweetest when
> you've known defeat."
> ~ Malcolm S Forbes

All of the planning and preparations served me very well for this event and I have only a few minor details to fine tweak before my next 111km overnight paddle.

The challenges were present and intense at times, but thankfully I remained calm and kept moving forward, focusing on executing my plan.

I have stressed the words 'commitment', 'consistency', 'confidence' and 'courage' as I wanted to encourage you to consider these elements in all that you do.

Especially if you decide to implement The Beginner

Blueprint into your life. It is these very elements that will become the back bone of your efforts and will hold the answer as to whether or not you will achieve your goals.

Here are some photos of the Hawkesbury Canoe Classic and a few memories of the race. Roy and I completed the race in the early hours of Sunday morning.

A huge thank you must go to our landcrew who worked throughout the night. There is no way that I would have had such a smooth and enriching experience without them. Thank you to Roy for keeping me company. A priceless experience with life changing rewards.

This first picture is of Roy, Robert and myself. This is Robert and Roy talking strategy. If you think I'm looking a little confused, then you guessed right. I tried to take in all their advice, but in the end I just followed the little red line on my GPS.

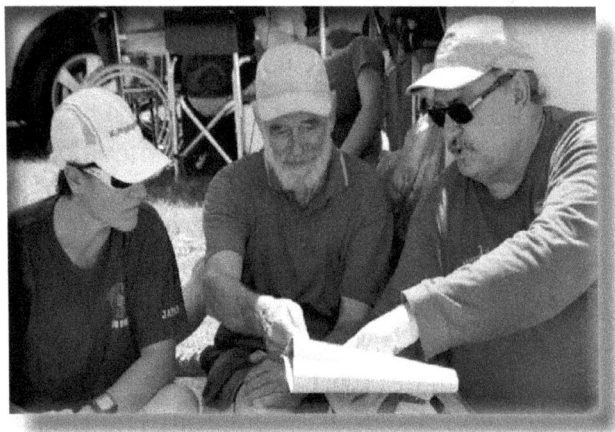

Here I am with a big grin from ear to ear expecting to be paddling with the tide for the first part of the race. I didn't get a favourable tide from the start, but I did get what seemed like a river of thick honey to paddle through.

Having to deal with the heat for the first part of the race and the thick river of honey, my posture collapsed. Although my breathing wasn't effected at this stage the weight of my drinking system on my back felt heavy.

Soon enough, my focus was on my hands. The coban tape wasn't too tight this time, but I had a lot more tape on than usual. The night before the race I picked up a hot saucepan and burned my hand. What was I thinking?

I was only minutes into the race and I could feel a battle going on within my mind. Thankfully I was aware of my thoughts and I had a plan as to how I was going to refocus myself.

I deliberately shifted my focus on to:
1. How I could help Roy
2. What I was grateful for
3. The magnificence of the Hawkesbury River

Before long I had pulled myself together. I had found a more effortless paddling rhythm which allowed me to enjoy Roy's company as we paddled down the Hawkesbury River together.

About half way through the race we were up against a storm which made our final kilometres to Wiseman's Ferry extremely challenging. I was feeling the fear kick in, but Roy was in a world of his own. The more the rain and wind intensified, he became more determined to push forward to our next check point.

When someone is running, you run with them. I made a quick decision to drop the 'fear game' and stepped it up with Roy. The way Roy moved his kayak through those waters was inspirational. I just wanted to stay by his side and enjoy this victory moment with him.

That one moment lifted my energy to overflowing and had me buzzing all the way through to our final land crew check point with great confidence. We paddled well together even if we couldn't find all of the check points the first time round.

The final stretch reminded me of the long drives from the Sunshine Coast to Newcastle with the kids. Are we there yet? It seemed to take forever. By now my body was starting to break down. My grazed body parts continued to rub and soak up the splashes of water leaving me in a whole lot of pain.

I decided to focus on my posture, breathing and keeping an even paddling rhythm. This really helped to take my mind off the pain and keep moving forward one stroke at a time.

I remember our final chat together as we approached the finish line. We were arguing about who should cross the line first. We both wanted to let the other person go ahead. In the end, we decided that we would cross together. We started together and we would finish together.

Story: Inspirational People

STAYING TRUE TO YOURSELF

A Great Role Model Doing Things Her Way

I have known this person for sometime. Julie has a similar story to that of Jordan. Julie's kids also attended our karate school and she later started a training program for herself.

Julie also demonstrates great determination, effort and enthusiasm. She inspires many of us to always give more of ourselves in our training and in our lives.

One of the things I love most about Julie is her ability to 'be herself.' Julie has had enough life experience to know who she is, what she likes and what she wants in her life.

Julie accepts herself with an awareness of all her perceived strengths and weaknesses. She chooses to nurture and develop herself continually as she moves towards achieving her goals.

As a result of this inner strength and self acceptance, Julie continues to amaze us with her results. People have often said to me in the past, that the truth is in your results. I can see this when I reflect on my time with Julie.

If somebody said to me that accepting yourself as you are would help me achieve my goals, I probably wouldn't have believed them when I was younger. With time, maturity and a little bit of wisdom, I'm starting to appreciate its power.

There is no other person exactly like Julie. Nobody will travel the same path in exactly the same way. Nobody will see and experience the world exactly like Julie. Julie's life is for her alone and it is up to her to make of it as she pleases.

There is no place for comparing or competing with others, as we are all so unique and equipped with a variety of gifts and different strengths and weaknesses.

We have all endured a variety of environments, relationships and experiences; all of which contribute to us becoming the people we are today.

I've observed Julie working on her own, and I've observed her working with others. I have observed Julie in a competitive environment, but not once have I seen her buying into comparing herself with others.

I have lost count of how many times somebody has quit an activity or given up on a goal because they were comparing themselves to somebody else.

Comparing and competing can have a crippling effect in your life and will rarely help you grow to your fullest potential. It will keep you from truly knowing yourself and the many gifts that you have within you.

There have been countless opportunities for Julie to compare herself with others. And, like us, maybe she has and still does from time to time.

But, rather than comparing herself to others, Julie seems to have an internal system which tracks her personal progress. When the green lights are flashing within this internal system, then all is good. There is no need to get caught up on the results and achievements of others.

She knows that she is progressing in her own way and in her own time, and that is all that matters.

MUSCLES FOR LIFE

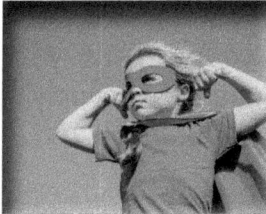

SELF ACCEPTANCE

As soon as you accept that you are already perfect and start loving yourself the way you are, you will be united with the most amazing person that you will ever meet.

This is the person that will be able to make all your dreams come true. Gently and surely, learn everything you can about yourself. It is in this knowing that you will realise your gifts and skills. You can then apply these gifts and skills to your life.

To help give you a better idea of knowing yourself and applying your gifts, consider your first time driving a car. You get in, there are lots of fancy controls and gadgets. You are going to need to learn what they do and how you will use them.

The more you learn about all of these controls and gadgets, the better your chances of driving your car well. The more you know about yourself and your gifts, the greater the chance of applying them to your life in a favourable way.

COMPARING AND COMPETING WITH OTHERS

Other people can be a great help to us in our lives. Yet, at times, we can allow people to indirectly take our personal power when we compare or compete with them. This may leave you in a highly non-productive and negative state with the feeling of not being good enough.

It can also sap your energy and enthusiasm so much that you lose sight of your goals. This can leave you in a place of 'waiting', where not a great deal happens.

If you stay in this waiting place for too long, life can start happening to you. This isn't always such a pleasant experience.

When you know yourself, your values and desires, you develop an inner strength. This inner strength replaces competing with others with competing with yourself.

When you compete with yourself, you are given a more accurate indication of your personal progress in all areas of your life.

PATIENCE

Whilst you are waiting to achieve your goal, how will you spend your time? One of the greatest currencies that we all receive is 24 hours of time per day.

The way that we spend our allocated time can make a big difference when it comes to achieving goals.

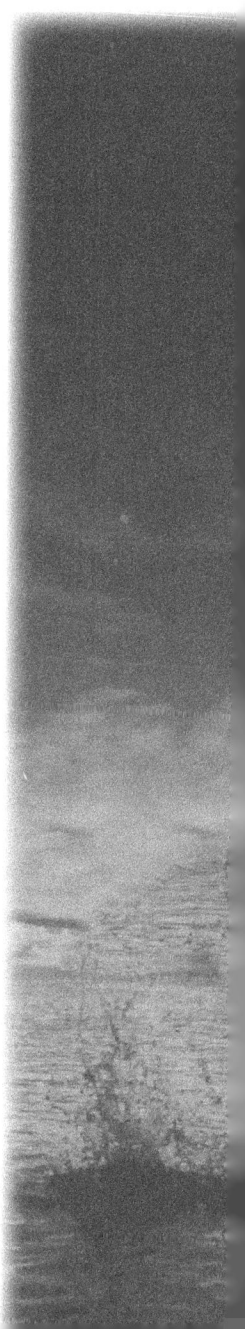

Chapter 3

REVEALING THE REWARDS

- Reflecting On A Great Journey
- Limiting Beliefs
- Serving Others
- *Story* - Inspirational People: A Great Student Will Always Attract Great Opportunities

Reflecting on a Great Journey

It's hard to believe that twelve months ago I would never have considered taking up paddling. If you looked at my goals, you wouldn't have seen paddling on my goals list. Yet, it has been one of the most remarkable adventures that I have ever enjoyed.

Not only did I enjoy the journey very much, I could feel myself being stretched and expanded out of my comfort zone every step of the way. The thing I loved the most was that I found myself predominantly focused on serving others.

Not only did I want to help Roy, but I also wanted to create a resource which may help others with achieving their goals. I've been very fortunate to experience some great results in karate, but I've never taken the time to pull the key lessons together in a written format.

With my focus on serving others, I found myself more able to be more positive and productive. Serving others also helped me with relaxing and enjoying the journey, as opposed to taking life too seriously.

Taking life too seriously never seems to end well for me. I've tried and tested this quality since childhood. I would easily experience fear, lose momentum and end up not being productive. It was during these times of taking life too seriously that I have contemplated giving up.

"Don't look any further than your own reflection for a hero."
~ Allyson Partridge

I believe that having the knowledge, experience, wisdom and perspective gained from my years of karate training, provided me with a solid foundation for this paddling adventure.

It is a foundation that I have nurtured and developed over a long period of time. It is a foundation that I'm

very grateful to have and it has saved me from myself countless times.

This adventure has given me a greater appreciation of many things. I had to pinch myself at one stage of this adventure when I was studying 'commitment', 'consistency', 'confidence' and 'courage'.

I never realised how powerful this combination was in my life up until now. The ideas featured in The Beginner Blueprint have been trapped within me for many years. I've been able to access ideas from this internal gold mine, yet I haven't been able to pull it together with clarity.

I'm really excited about exploring The Beginner Blueprint further as I commit to future adventures. There is still a great deal more I can do with my understanding and application of the ideas presented in The Beginner Blueprint.

The Results Are In
The physical result that you can see - I completed a 111km overnight paddle along side of Roy.

The internal result that can't be seen - My very foundations of my life (muscles for life) have strengthened. My confidence is developing and propelling me forward to even greater adventures. With this growth from within, I am able to access greater peace, love, joy and harmony.

Limiting Beliefs

As a result of this experience I have since been reviewing my goals with a new perspective. Prior to completing the 111km paddle, I believed that there was no way that I could have done it. Especially given my starting point.

So, it's got me asking the questions, what else am I saying that I can't do just yet? Is it all in my mind? If I was to just make a commitment and apply The Beginner Blueprint coupled with commitment, consistency, confidence and courage, maybe I could work towards some of those goals now.

"Your imagination is your preview of life's coming attractions." ~ Albert Einstein

I think this is one piece of reflection that has left me with a whole lot of curiosity. My time studying karate has been a powerful force shaping me to this very day. But, what else could I really achieve now that I have collated all the pieces of the puzzle shared in The Beginner Blueprint?

And more importantly, what are **you** saying that you can't do right now? Could you welcome The Beginner Blueprint into your life, and break through those limiting beliefs and fears that may exist?

63

Serving Others

The 111km paddling adventure all came about because of a discussion after dinner one night with Roy. I believe my focus on helping him with this race ended up helping me more. Not only with my preparations, but also throughout the race and now with the lessons that I take away from this experience.

I remember paddling by Roy's side and encouraging him to keep his rhythm and just keep moving consistently. With every positive word of encouragement that I thought and spoke to him, I felt it fuel my very being. It was as if the words fuelled Roy and then bounced back and fuelled me simultaneously.

"Success has nothing to do with what you gain in life or accomplish for yourself. It's what you do for others." ~ Danny Thomas

This injection of energy is something that I feel quite regularly when I teach at our karate school. I guess it is such a familiar environment that I take it for granted and I haven't given it much thought in the past.

I can go to our karate school feeling tired but this level of energy rarely stays. If I enter the dojo and truly put everything into serving others, I receive an energy hit which gets me through to the end and more.

The times when I am feeling the worst, require greater intent to focus on serving others. Yet, it is these classes that end up being the most productive with a great balance of fun and focus.

It is only in participating in a different environment, with different people, that I have been able to really appreciate this energy that I receive every day in my life.

When you do what you love, and you find yourself being of value to others, you can feel your energy being lifted. Maybe you could liken it to your very own energy bank account.

With every act of genuine service to another person, you are being gifted with energy. Not only are you being gifted with energy, you are also being gifted with the personal growth, the people, and the resources that you will need to help you achieve your goals.

Story: Inspirational People

A GREAT STUDENT WILL ALWAYS ATTRACT GREAT OPPORTUNITIES

Learning Wholeheartedly and Always Giving the Best of Himself

From day one, Blake has demonstrated a whole lot of passion, enthusiasm and a large amount of action. In terms of passion, I cannot remember a time when Blake has given anything but his best. Ever!!!

Year after year, he consistently turns up at the dojo and gives 100% effort. When you give Blake a task, he takes it on board with great pleasure, energy and curiosity.

He breaks the task down into little pieces, puts it all back together piece by piece, until he arrives at a point of feeling satisfied. Then he moves onto the next task and so on.

Blake revisits these same tasks time and time again. He'll break the task down, explore, dig deeper and put it all back together in an even more spectacular way.

Blake has clearly found an activity (karate) which he can really sink his teeth into and bring out his best. It is also evident that he is quite comfortable in the learning environment, and very trusting of the guidance that he receives.

There are times when he simply doesn't understand where he is being led, and there are times when progress can seem slow. No matter what, he continues to step forward one lesson at a time trusting his instructors.

He allows his instructors to do what they do best. He then takes the information and practises to the best of his ability, returning with questions if needed.

All of these qualities and more, have set Blake up for sizeable success in a very short time frame. One of the greatest lessons that I have taken from Blake, is how his effort as a student has positioned him to be a great leader.

Blake also gives his time to help others. He understands the importance of sharing knowledge and not keeping it locked away on the inside. The combination of learning and sharing will serve Blake well as he continues to grow as both a student and a leader.

MUSCLES FOR LIFE

PASSION

You'll know when you are passionate about something. You'll always be thinking, doing and talking about it.

For example, my daughter has a growing passion for gymnastics. It doesn't matter where she is, she'll be twisting herself inside out, doing hand stands, cart wheels and flips.

I find her watching gymnastic videos on YouTube quite regularly these days. She has set up a YouTube channel of her own, and she keeps her little brother busy trying to twist and tie himself in a knot.

If you know you aren't doing what you love, see what you can do to identify your passion in life. If you are doing what you love, then do more of it.

Grow the passion within you so much that you are overflowing. In time and in your own way, share your passion with others.

COMFORTABLE LEARNING ENVIRON-MENT TO BRING OUT YOUR BEST

For me the karate dojo is an ideal learning environment. Over the years, I have invested a large amount of time into this environment. The more time I have invested as a student, the more comfortable I have become.

When I started to give my time to help others, I felt valued and appreciated. Soon enough I developed a sense of belonging which encouraged greater comfort.

By investing your time into a communtiy of like minded people, you can establish a level of comfort and trust which allows you to be more natural and relaxed.

If you truly feel comfortable in your learning environment, you'll be better equipped to deal with all results that you achieve. You'll also have a greater chance of becoming the best version of you in all areas of your life.

TRUSTING THE GUIDANCE OF THOSE BEFORE YOU

I have a karate teacher that has been training and teaching for more than 60 years. I don't question the path that he is taking me on, I just trust it is the perfect path for me.

There are times of frustration and not understanding what I'm doing, or where I am meant to be going. I don't know what is before me, but I trust that he does and that he'll guide me accordingly.

If I'm being guided in a certain direction, I'll always aim to receive the guidance and practise. I'll dig as deep as I can on my own and I'll follow up with questions as required.

If I have ever wanted to grow in a certain way, I've always looked to see who is doing what I want to achieve. I've learned that it is much easier and more efficient to trust the experts.

I've also learned to avoid 'assuming' that I know everything. There is a reason why the experts are experts in their chosen fields.

Chapter 4

THE BEGINNER BLUEPRINT

- A Thought On The Path To Achieving Your Goals
- Story - Inspirational People: A Shift In Perspective Could Be All That Is Needed
- The Beginner Blueprint Overview
- Breaking Down The Beginner Blueprint
- Leading By Example
- Story - Inspirational People: All Interactions Begin And End With Respect

A Thought on The Path To Achieving Your Goals

The Beginner Blueprint, if applied well to your life, will help you achieve your goals, big or small. I'm not suggesting that it will be easy, but it is simple. Just because it is simple, please don't dismiss it.

I'm not suggesting that it will be quick, but you will arrive at your destination at the perfect time for you. You may not hit your target the first time, but simply re-assess and recommit to your goals.

"Yesterday is history, Tomorrow is a mystery, Today is a gift, that is why it is called the present."
~ Unknown

You will notice with The Beginner Blueprint, that you will need to take full responsibility when it comes to achieving your goals.

By all means, please seek guidance from those who have travelled the path before you. They will be able to help you set realistic target dates, and share resources that may help you.

Before getting into The Beginner Blueprint, there is just one final thought that I would like to share with you. I hope this thought will make a difference when you proceed with your goal setting. Compare these two pictures illustrating the path from start to finish when pursuing your goals.

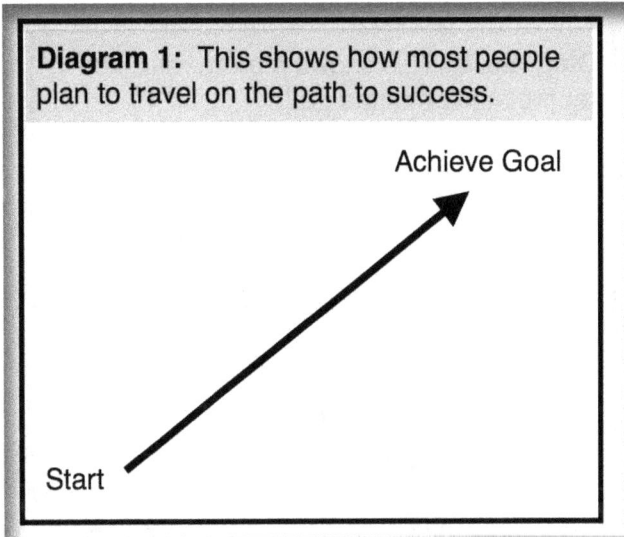

Diagram 1: This shows how most people plan to travel on the path to success.

Achieve Goal

Start

The first picture is often what some people expect to experience when setting goals. It is a smooth path, with no challenges. Unfortunately, when you come across a bump in the road, you can be in for an emotional roller coaster ride.

This emotional roller coaster ride is driven by the force and frustration of a person desperately wanting to achieve their goals. The more force and frustration, the greater chance of fatigue and feelings of discouragement.

In my experience, the second picture, is a more accurate illustration of what to expect when you set out to achieve your goals.

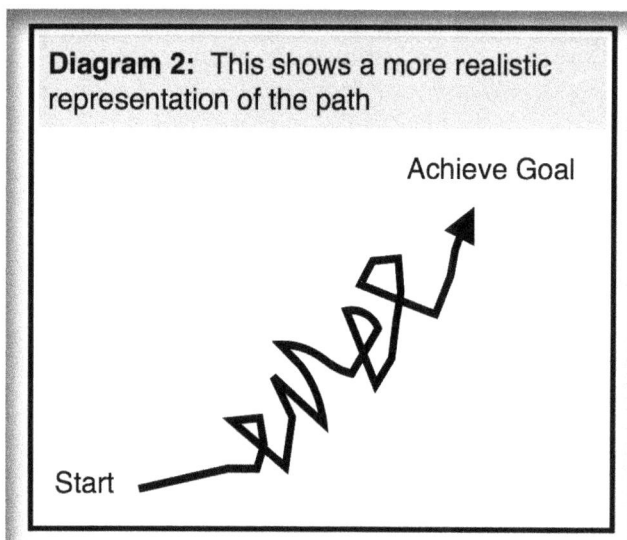

Diagram 2: This shows a more realistic representation of the path

Achieve Goal

Start

In order to achieve some of our goals we need to first grow ourselves. This can and does include 'growing pains'. We are stretched and expanded out of our comfort zone. It is the presence of these 'growing pains', that will lead us to developing the right mindset and the tools to achieve our goals.

If you are aware from the beginning that you will have some 'growing pains', you can better develop your way of thinking. You may even come to the realisation that everything is perfect. You just need to find and understand the lessons within each experience.

You may not be able to control everything that happens in your life, but you can choose how to respond to things in your life. Choose to find the gift in every experience. After all, it is these very experiences that determine who you are today, and who you will become.

If you have big goals, expect to attract potentially big and confronting experiences. These experiences will help you develop the skills that you need to achieve your goals. For some of us, this will feel like the end of the world at times.

To find the best of ourselves, we need to break away all that is no longer required and renew our minds, bodies and spirits. This process can equip you with all that you need to achieve your goals and more.

Be patient with yourself and never rush or force the learning process. In the perfect time, you'll mature in a way which will enable you to embrace and receive your goal. Be grateful for all experiences. Without them, there is a good chance that you may not receive what you need in order to achieve your goals.

If you reflect deeply on your life, you may have noticed how there may have been some personal challenges prior to achieving a goal. Often, it isn't until years later that you appreciate those challenges.

No matter what, just hang in there. If you want to stack the odds in your favour, find a purpose that is bigger than you. This will keep you on track even

when you are fatigued. This is what my commitment to Roy did for me.

Once I committed, it was like walking into a room and closing the door behind me. Just to make sure there was no going back, I deliberately locked the door and threw away the key. Now, I only had one option, and that was to move forward. That is what commitment means to me.

When you position yourself in this way, where there is only one way to move forward, everything will start to align itself for you. It may feel as though your world has been turned upside down. But, choose to stay positive and trust that your world is being aligned in the perfect way to help you achieve your goals.

Story: Inspirational People

A SHIFT IN PERSPECTIVE COULD BE ALL THAT IS NEEDED

A Magical Perspective

Although I seem to be surrounding myself with many people with a great perspective on life, I want to share with you the first person that comes to mind when I think about perspective. Her name is Rebecca and no matter what is going on, 'everything is all good.'

I'm not saying that she doesn't get her fair share of challenges, but she believes that everything is happening for a reason and all will be good. Rebecca meets adversity with a calm, accepting and peaceful heart.

I've had conversations with Rebecca over these last few years about her challenges. Not once has she ever complained or blamed another person for her circumstances. If anything, she receives each circumstance with gratitude.

Rebecca simply assesses the challenge at hand and does her best to do what she can with the things in her control. The things that are out of her control, she aims to let go, although for all of us, this can be difficult.

Rebecca is an amazing young mum with a beautiful family. She also finds the time to operate a successful business with her husband. Together as a team, this family has achieved so much.

Rebecca's wisdom and knowledge is remarkable. Her ability to trust and have faith in the processes of life is truly beautiful and admirable.

I've had the pleasure to work with Rebecca at our karate school for sometime now. It has been truly inspiring watching her grow in confidence. When she enters the dojo these days, it is game on.

Rebecca is there to work. She pushes the boundaries with every lesson and takes complete responsibility for her results. Rebecca also has her kids train with us at our karate school.

I love seeing more and more parents step up and lead by example in the dojo. I especially love seeing kids watch their parents in action.

The smiles on their face say it all. 'That's my mum (dad)!' You can see how proud they are of their parents. Actions seem to speak louder than words. Parents can tell their kids how to live, or they can step up and show them how to live.

MUSCLES FOR LIFE

PERSPECTIVE

You may already have a great perspective on life, but continue to learn and develop your perspective. The smallest refinement to our 'muscles for life' can make a huge difference in our results.

Monitor your thoughts regularly and see how you can further refine your thoughts to produce better results in your life.

Take the time to slow down each day and reward yourself with time to breathe well. Take the time to think of all the things you are grateful for in your life. Identify ways you can put a smile on someone's face with no expectation of anything in return.

FULL RESPONSIBILITY FOR YOURSELF

When you take responsibility for your circumstances, you can tune into your skills and gifts to create a more favourable outcome.

When you blame others you instantly give up access to your own skills and gifts. This may result in a feeling of helplessness.

We often go through life wanting a miracle. As soon as you realise that you are the miracle in your life, magic will happen.

A little bit at a time, choose to take greater responsibility for yourself and your results. Learn about you. You are the greatest person that you will ever meet. You are the one person equipped with all that you need to live the life of your dreams.

CONTROLLABLE AND UNCONTROLLABLE

In life there are things that you can control and things that you can't control. Identify what you can control. Assess the situation and based on your goals, make a decision on how to move forward.

Things that you have no control over; let them go. Many of us get caught up on things that are out of our control. We can waste a lot of energy being upset with things that we cannot change. When you hold onto these things you can find yourself in a real mess emotionally.

Learn about yourself and develop strategies that allow you to let go of anything out of your control. At the end of the day, it is only going to disturb your inner peace and eat you up on the inside.

PEACE

No matter what you may be experiencing in life, consider seeking peace. Look for peace within yourself, your relationships and with the processes of life. Seeking peace will help you to gain a greater appreciation of life.

"Peace begins with a smile."
~ Mother Teresa

The Beginner Blueprint Overview

On the next page you can see an overview of The Beginner Blueprint. You may have already noticed elements of The Beginner Blueprint scattered throughout earlier chapters of this book. Now you can see the blueprint in its entirety.

"If 'plan A' didn't work. The alphabet has 25 more letters! Stay cool." ~ Unknown

In chapter one, you were introduced briefly to *'goal setting basics'* and *'create a plan'* sections of The Beginner Blueprint. Within the *'Inspirational People Stories'* and my own recollections of my 111km paddle (preparations and race), I've revealed a few of the *'muscles for life'.*

Whether you have been developing a plan of your own whilst reading The Beginner Blueprint or not, I hope the overview on the next page helps give you greater clarity. The combination of the three key elements of The Beginner Blueprint, will accelerate your efforts towards achieving your goals.

Let's now look more closely at 'goal setting basics' and 'creating a plan' within the next section, 'Breaking Down The Beginner Blueprint'.

THE Beginner BLUEPRINT

"Goals are dreams with deadlines." ~ Unknown

"A goal without a plan is just a wish." ~ Unknown

"Nothing worth having comes easy." ~ Unknown

GOAL SETTING BASICS

1. Choose a goal (including target date)
2. Make a commitment (including an action)
3. Awareness of starting point
4. Achieving your goal. How will it help you? How will it help others?

CREATE A PLAN

1. Establish a timeline
2. Listen and learn
3. Self awareness
4. Familiarity of equipment/tools
5. Positive fuel
6. Familiarity of environment
7. Support team
8. Pre-event rehearsals
9. Immersion
10. Measuring progress

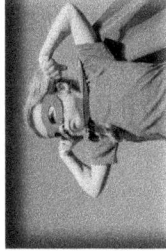

MUSCLES FOR LIFE

Exercise these muscles daily to give you the best chance to achieve your goals. Consider adding other qualities.

Consistent effort, self discipline, perseverance, patience, focus, commitment, respect, trust, gratitude, imagination, love, peace, go with the flow, positive perspective, do your best, help others, 100% responsibility for you.

Breaking Down The Beginner Blueprint

In this section we'll go through each of the key elements of The Beginner Blueprint.

"The secret of getting ahead
is getting started."
~ Unknown

If you can understand the elements of The Beginner Blueprint with a touch of perspective, it will stack the odds in your favour when it comes to applying it to your life. Let's get started.

GOAL SETTING BASICS

1. **CHOOSE A GOAL (INCLUDING TARGET DATE)**
2. **MAKE A COMMITMENT (ACTION)**
3. **AWARENESS OF YOUR STARTING POINT**

When you make a decision to commit to something, you will instantly gain a sense of clarity. Especially if you have a target date, an awareness of your starting point and you have your first actions in place.

When you commit to a goal, you give your mind a purpose. It's not unusual that you'll find yourself thinking a lot more about your goal.

Your immediate focus is to get the wheels turning and gain some momentum towards your goal. One of my favourite ways to do this, is to simply draw two boxes side by side on a blank piece of A4 paper (landscape). Link these two boxes up with three action steps that you can act on straight away.

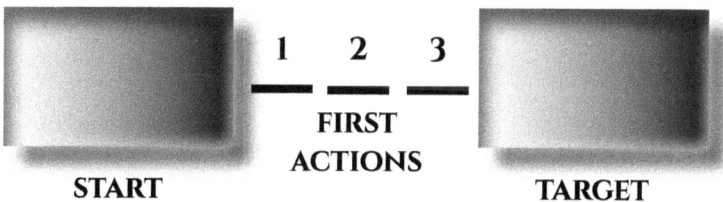

1   2   3

FIRST ACTIONS

START

TARGET

Give your goal some thought, then see if you can add information to each section.

TARGET: Collect information about your goal, including target dates. You may also include some check-in points along the way. These are especially valuable if you have a goal which may take months or years to achieve.

START: Collect information about your starting point. This will highlight your strengths and weaknesses. It will also bring to your attention any resources, prior knowledge or people that may be able to help you.

FIRST ACTIONS: Hit the ground running and start taking action straight away. This will create even greater thought and will open doors of opportunity. When implementing your actions, choose a pace that you can maintain over an extended period of time.

When opportunities arise, simply build on your actions list. Commit to consistent effort and be flexible as you move towards your goal.

MUSCLES FOR LIFE

MOMENTUM

Imagine a wheel that moves from your 'start box' to your 'target box'. The only way to move the wheel is through your actions.

For as long as you continue to take action, your wheel will move towards your target. It may not always go in a straight line, but it will be moving. Be patient and allow yourself to embrace the processes of learning.

Learning involves a good amount of testing and measuring but in the end, you'll find the alignment required to achieve your goal.

If you string together a lot of actions over a longer period of time, you will have the potential to gain greater momentum. In turn, you will accelerate the speed at which you move the wheel forward. The absence of action, will have your wheel come to a complete stop.

Always remember that it's easier to move a wheel which is already in motion and has momentum. It's harder to move a wheel that has come to a complete stop. Do all that you can to keep moving forward one day at a time.

GOAL SETTING BASICS

4. IN ACHIEVING YOUR GOAL, HOW WILL IT HELP YOU? HOW WILL IT HELP OTHERS?

Although it is great to be aware of how the attainment of our goals will serve us, I've found that it isn't such a great practice to keep this at the forefront of our minds.

After many years of studying myself and others, I've noticed that people generally perform better when they are not focused on themselves.

When we focus on ourselves we will often become self-conscious and worry about things that are out of our control. This generally leads to a build up of fear, a negative state of mind and low productivity.

"Great achievement is usually born of great sacrifice; and is never the result of selfishness."
~ Napoleon Hill

When we commit to new goals quietly to ourselves, it is easy to give up with the onset of 'growing pains'. No one will have ever known about your goal, so you won't be seen as a failure. Please also be careful with this method of goal setting.

88

Every time you give up, you are indirectly losing your personal power and reducing your confidence levels. You are also welcoming the habit of 'giving up' when things get tough. The more you fuel this habit, the more you may experience the feeling of being worthless in your life.

Although outwardly nobody will know of your broken commitment, inwardly you will know. Over time, these broken commitments build up and before you know it, you will have the fight of your life. Some of the physical signs I've noticed within myself at my greatest times of need include the following:

- change in posture (more closed, shoulders forward and slumped appearance)
- eyes lowered and often avoiding eye contact
- shallow breathing
- low energy and fatigued
- negative self talk (unable to find the good)
- depression, anxiety
- sleepless nights
- isolating oneself

Something else I've discovered, is that many of us will sooner step out of our comfort zones to help another person before we'll help ourselves. How many parents reading this have spent countless days providing for the needs of their families and have ignored their own needs?

I read recently that we aren't wired to solve our own problems, but we are wired to help others solve their

problems. This is something that I'm seeing more and more in my own life. This is why I'm encouraging you to consider helping others. Find a reason to succeed that is bigger than you.

> ### "We rise by lifting others."
> ### ~ Unknown

When a person asks you for help, how do you feel? My first feeling is, wow!! My time and presence is of value to another person. We all like to feel needed and valued. When we are given these opportunities to help others, we indirectly grow ourselves.

I love helping people achieve their goals. It is one of the most energising things that I get to do. The act of helping others takes my full focus and helps me live in the moment. This is the place in which I enter a state of greater productivity. I also attract the experiences, people and resources that I need to achieve my own goals.

Here is another great reason why we should consider helping others. Have you ever realised how brave we can be when we are doing things for others?

There is no way I would have tried a 111km overnight paddle if it was for my own benefit. That would just be insane, especially given my starting point and associated fears.

As I was focused on helping Roy, I found it easy to put on a brave face and go head to head with my fears.

I hope that you can see the value and positive impact of having your focus on helping others at the forefront of your mind. You can, and will, achieve your goals and more.

Allow yourself to be of service to others whilst simultaneously having a clear goal to pursue. Not only will you benefit in your own life with each goal that you achieve, but you will also add great value to the lives of others.

MUSCLES FOR LIFE

LIFE BASICS

Before putting the act of helping others at the forefront of your mind, it is important that you have considered your *'Life Basics'*.

'Life Basics', are things that fuel you in a positive way. Your aim is to fuel yourself well everyday. When you are feeling great, you will be able to better help others and, in turn, move towards achieving your goals.

'Life Basics' include things like: food, water, sleep, air, self care, rest, movement, sun, family and relationships.

Take the time now to review your goal. Consider why your goal is important to you. If your 'why' is big enough, you won't have too much trouble with keeping yourself focused and staying motivated.

In achieving this goal:
1. What are the benefits to you?
2. How will it help others?

PLAN

CREATE A PLAN

Leading up to your target date, aim to test, measure and refine the key elements presented below.

1. ESTABLISH A TIME LINE
Refer back to your A4 landscape piece of paper with your target date, starting point and first actions.

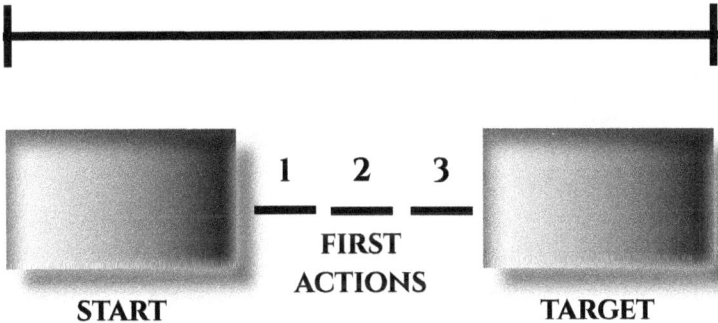

1 2 3
FIRST
ACTIONS

START   **TARGET**

At the top of the page, draw a horizontal line as I have done above. This will be your 'time line'. The far left vertical line, is your start date. The far right vertical line, is your target date.

You may not have too many details at this stage, but see if you can add other significant dates to this time-line. It may include things like: short term goals, full dress rehearsals, training intensity adjustments, rest periods, meetings and check-in dates, deadlines to complete sections of a larger project.

93

When I create my timelines, I like to start with the end in mind. This is just a personal preference. There have been times when I haven't achieved my goal by my target dates. There have also been times when I have missed my short term goals.

If you experience these kinds of results, simply take the time to revisit your timeline and re-commit to your goal. As a teenager, I had a goal of becoming a karate world champion. It took four attempts and a total of fourteen years to achieve this goal.

"Fall down seven times,
stand up eight."
~ Japanese proverb

2. LISTEN AND LEARN

When I first started paddling, there wasn't a session which I didn't end up with a grazed bottom. This went on for months. My tail bone just didn't seem to like any of the kayak seats that were available.

Our ocean skis were even worse. I grew more and more disheartened throughout that period of testing and measuring. Martin and I tried everything from creams, padding, sheep skin, paddle pants etc

We researched marathon paddlers via the internet, and spoke to people who were experienced long distance paddlers to no avail.

Eventually, we found a marathon paddler who had similar issues with seating. He recommended a certain kind of camping mattress. To look at this camping mattress, I must admit I was skeptical that it would work. But, we cut it up and threw a piece into the ocean skis and haven't looked back.

Although we spent a lot of time researching, testing and measuring, we eventually found a paddler that shared almost identical issues with their seating. We are all a little bit different, and it can take time to find the solution that fits your specific circumstances.

Keep seeking out experts who are doing what you want to do. Listen, learn and try things. Eventually something will meet your needs.

When you look at your goal, can you identify experts that may be able to guide you? Do you know anyone that has achieved the results that you want to achieve? Start connecting with these people.

3. SELF AWARENESS
You are your greatest asset. So, prioritise learning more about you, and choose to build the foundations of your life.

The more you can learn about you, the better able you are to direct yourself to achieve a more favourable result. If you were driving a car for the first time, you would take the time to learn more about your vehicle, before heading out for your first driving experience.

The same is true for your mind and body. Take the time to become more aware of you. You have a powerful mind and body. You are capable of creating the life of your dreams.

To help with developing your self awareness, I'd highly recommend that you seek out experts that can guide you on this journey of self discovery. Although you may move from one adventure to another, choose to commit to an ongoing self development program.

To help with your self development be sure to check out the A Way of Living, "Design Your Life and Enjoy Purposeful Living Guide." Within this guide, I walk you through a series of steps to eventually create a plan for your life, which will deeply resonate with your heart. This plan will increase your life, and help you enjoy greater clarity, creativity, calmness, confidence and contribution in your life.

When you have yourself operating at a peak state, you will be able to give more of yourself to achieve your goals.

4. FAMILIARITY OF EQUIPMENT/TOOLS

In the case of my 111km overnight paddle, I wanted to know that prior to competition day, I was confident and comfortable with all equipment. I created equipment checklists for my training sessions. Later, I also created checklists for my landcrew on competition day.

I used all equipment often in both relaxed and pressure situations. After a while of becoming familiar with my equipment, I soon learned that it may be worthwhile having spares of some items available on race day just in case. Things like extra clothing, batteries for GPS, taping, hats etc

Your equipment can either stack the odds in your favour or distract you from achieving your goals. I remember competing at an international karate tournament where I loaned my chest guard to a team member.

As it worked out, I was called up whilst my team mate was competing in another competition area. I ended up borrowing somebody else's gear. Before I knew it, my match was over.

I had spent my entire match being distracted and feeling uncomfortable with my chest guard. My range of motion was limited, leaving me unable to execute my favourite techniques.

Take the time to consider what equipment that you may require to achieve your goals. Are you confident and comfortable with your equipment? How can you become more confident and comfortable with your equipment?

Consider ways to take care of your equipment and keep it in great condition. You want to know that your equipment is going to be reliable.

5. POSITIVE FUEL
Something that I have come to appreciate in my life, is that all experiences, environments and people are either fuelling you positively or negatively.

Because of my fears and lack of experience with paddling, I chose to keep a close eye on many fuel sources. I felt vulnerable, especially in the first six months preparing for my adventure. In my mind, I had a high probability of not following through with my 111km overnight paddle.

To give myself every chance possible to complete this adventure, I took the time to revisit the little things in my life. It was these litttle things that I did each day, which had the potential to get me across the finish line.

"Success consists of doing the common things of life uncommonly well." ~ Unknown

I mentioned 'life basics' a little earlier in this chapter. My key life basics include, food, water, sleep, air, self care, rest, movement, sun, family and relationships.

Over a period of eleven weeks, I explored my life basics (week one to week nine), environments (week ten) and experiences (week eleven). Each week, I would focus on just one element and I would write my findings in my journal. I didn't try to change anything, it was more a case of developing an awareness of my existing habits.

By the end of the eleven weeks, I had a listing of my positive and negative fuel sources for each element. I also had some action steps in place to implement at a pace that worked for me.

Soon, I'll give you an idea how I collected information and how I used it to get more out of the little things in my life.

STEP 1: DEVELOPING AWARENESS

Choose one of the following elements. You will deliberately give attention to this element daily for a period of one week. Food, water, sleep, air, self care, rest, movement, sun, family, relationships, environments, experiences.

Let's say I have chosen 'food' as a starting point. I would write down everything that I ate each day in my journal for one week. You can extend this further and include timing of meals, feelings about food, habits, food related education and discussions, meal preparation (home made, takeaway) etc.

If this is a new activity for you, I would keep it simple with one or two things to track. Each time you revisit this exercise, consider going a little deeper and seek further information about this element in your life.

As you improve your awareness, you'll be able to better understand and make refinements to this element in your life. With continual refinements of each element, you'll be able to see how the little things in your life can make a big difference.

STEP 2: POSITIVE OR NEGATIVE

Decide which journal entries are positive or negative. Next to journal entries write *'positive'* or *'negative'*. I like to use highlighters to highlight what is positive and negative. I find it faster when I am transferring information to the next step.

STEP 3: THE BIGGER PICTURE

At the end of the week, create the following template either on your computer or an A4 piece of paper. This template is only to give you a starting point. I've added some sample information to help get you started.

ELEMENT:	'Food'

POSITIVE

1. fruit - daily
2. vegetables - daily
3. home cooked meals Monday - Thursday

NEGATIVE

1. eating before bed
2. eating on the run - snacking in morning
3. afternoon - feeling crazy hungry, 3:00pm to bed

GRATITUDE (1-3 THINGS)

1. access to a variety of fresh foods each day
2. electricity and facilities to cook meals
3. eating with my family

MAKING A CHANGE (1-3 ACTION STEPS)

1. sit down meal at breakfast - take time to enjoy
2. cook larger quantities when cooking. Last a couple of nights. = home cooked meals most nights

The samples given within the template are only few and brief. Be sure to be as thorough as you can with the process. It will give you some great information about you and your habits. It will also align you to a greater way of living.

The key to this process is what you choose to do with the information. When I have tried to force myself into a new habit, I have rarely succeeded.

Yet, when I have deliberately focused my attention on something for a period of time with the desire to understand, I would welcome positive change into my life. The changes would be more natural and smooth.

My results have varied. I would say that I have made a lot of mistakes, but when you roll with the punches in a flowing way, everything seems to align in the perfect way and in the perfect time.

Why give gratitude? When you focus on what you are grateful for and when you find the good in all areas of your life, you shift your energy to a more positive state of energy.

If you are ever feeling lacking or negative with any elements, choose to focus your attention on 'finding the good' and 'gratitude'.

"It is not happy people who are thankful. It is thankful people who are happy." ~ Unknown

6. FAMILIARITY WITH ENVIRONMENT

When it comes to competing in karate tournaments, I've always appreciated the opportunity to visit the tournament venue before competition day. If there is any set up taking place in the days before, I'll happily volunteer so I can get a feel for the venue.

The more I can learn, the more I can relax and enjoy the competition. Otherwise, things can come up and distract me from executing my game plan.

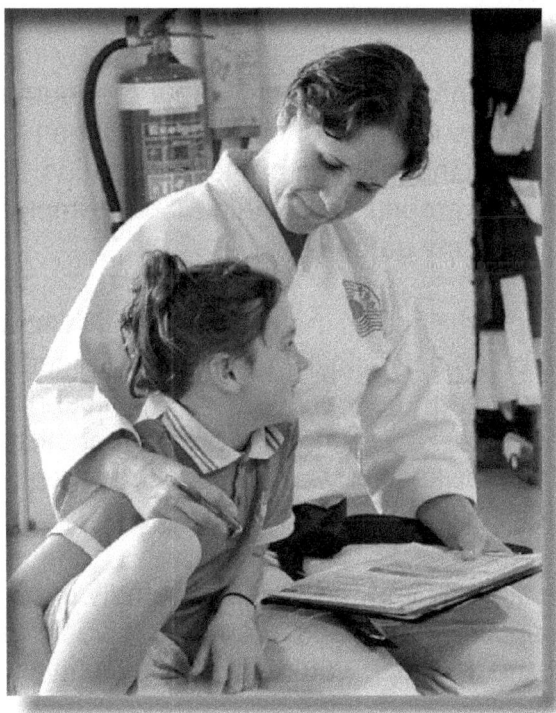

I like to gather as much information as I can about the tournament venue. I review things like transport to venue, size of the arena, team seating area, competition area, warm up area, condition of the competition mats, toilet and change rooms, shops at the venue and shops surrounding the venue.

"The distance between your dreams and reality is called action." ~ Unknown

Taking the time to learn more about the tournament venue, allows me to feel comfortable when I enter the venue on the morning of the competition. I don't need to rush around for anything. I can simply focus on executing my game plan.

Becoming familiar with the Hawkesbury River, wasn't going to be an option this time round. I needed to rely on my paddling experiences from my local rivers. I also needed to rely on the experiences of other paddlers, The Hawkesbury Canoe Classic event booklets and website.

Despite all that I learned, I was extremely uncomfortable about doing the race overnight. It was meant to be a full moon, which would have lit up the river beautifully.

Unfortunately, there was no moon, and in some parts of the river we were in complete darkness. I remember paddling and finding paddlers who had stopped paddling as they couldn't see where to go.

Thankfully, I'd had a couple of night time paddles before my big race. I'd even had the opportunity to paddle with no moon. That was a great chance to see how dark things may get on the Hawkesbury River.

As it worked out, we invested in a GPS to help settle my nerves. Martin helped me set up our GPS to include all the check points and I just followed the red line on the screen.

One of my landcrew, Rod, also had a tracking device. We attached this tracking device to my ocean ski, so my land crew knew exactly where I was and how fast I was travelling.

With these two gadgets and Roy by my side, I felt comfortable, safe and confident to make my way up the beautiful Hawkesbury River. Even when we were greeted with a lightning show and rain, I still felt calm and able to focus on every stroke.

In reflection, although I wasn't able to experience the Hawkesbury River environment first hand, I was able to access education and technology to give me a sense of familiarity and confidence with the environment.

Now, take a look at your goal. In order for you to achieve your goals, consider the environments which you may need to learn more about. The more comfortable, focused and productive you can be in these environments, the better your chances of achieving a positive result.

7. SUPPORT TEAM

Behind every great adventure there is usually a team of people helping to bring about the best possible result for everyone involved. I was extremely fortunate to receive a great deal of help on this adventure.

Every person involved in this adventure was of great value. There is no way that I would have completed twelve months of preparations and then go on to complete the 111km overnight paddle without them.

My support team kept me accountable and kept it fun. They also provided a great deal of effort throughout this adventure, which allowed me to focus on paddling. There was no problem too big. It was simply straight to problem solving mode and discovering a way to move forward.

I remember pulling into my first major stop of the race and my ability to steer was deteriorating. My pedals lost responsiveness after hitting a big log in the water. Martin and Rod were brilliant.

I don't know what they did, but they sorted the problem with the cables and got me going in quick time. I felt like a racing car driver pulling in for a change of tyres and fuel and I was off again.

Roy was a great support person as well. At one stage of the paddle we were going with the tide. We were sitting on about 10km/hr and my speed quickly declined to about 4km/hr. No matter how much effort I put into every stroke, I couldn't get my speed up.

As it worked out, my rudder was loaded up with weed. We had problems with the weed protector that we purchased, so Roy was a real gentleman and pulled the weeds from my rudder every so often.

Martin's brother Robert was especially encouraging throughout the entire adventure. He had paddled this race a few times and was very open to share all that he knew to help me. We had countless hours on

the phone leading up to the race. On race day, Robert sat with us and reviewed the course and offered some great advice.

Rod and Luc were extremely generous with their time, knowledge and equipment. I remember pulling up to our second check point in the race in the early hours of the morning. We were greeted by Rod and Luc, knee deep in the water. I was cold sitting on my ocean ski paddling. I could only imagine how they were feeling standing around in the water.

"Alone we can do so little; together we can do so much."
~ Helen Keller

Martin was my rock throughout this entire adventure. When I was weak he offered strength. When I was confused he offered clarity. When I had doubt he offered hope. He always knew exactly what to do for me, even though there were times when I didn't graciously receive his help.

I've only shared a few stories here, but there are so many more examples of the help I received from my support team. From my early days learning how to paddle, to the many hours on the water with my training partner Bob. Not to mention all the sponsors who gave generously to help raise money for charity.

I have to also mention the team of volunteers at the Hawkesbury Canoe Classic. There was support at every corner you turned on the river. They were energetic, friendly, understanding and patient. The atmosphere at the main check points was overflowing with a great spirit and energy.

My support team were super positive and encouraging. Their combined knowledge, skills and energy ensured that I crossed the finish line. I really could not have asked for a more perfect support team.

Below are a few activities to help you create a support team to help you achieve your goals. I've given a few sample answers based on my 111km paddling race.

STEP 1: PERSONAL EVALUATION
Identify your goal, strengths and weaknesses.

GOAL: Complete 111km overnight paddle

STRENGTHS	WEAKNESSES
1. health, fitness	1. technology
2. flexibility of schedule to put in hours on the water	2. tail bone, lower back
3. self discipline	3. fears
4. prior knowledge	4. lack confidence in paddling environment

STEP 2: GOAL EVALUATION

To achieve your goal, what are some of the main tasks that need to happen?

GOAL: Complete 111km overnight paddle

1. Personal development, dealing with fears and anxiety in paddling envrionment
2. Ability to paddle 111km
3. Researching and collecting equipment
4. Ocean ski maintenance
5. Technology fixtures and fittings
6. Nutrition research
7. Landcrew manager, ability to drive car with trailer

STEP 3: IDENTIFY TASKS FOR YOU

Based on your strengths and weaknesses (step 1), identify what tasks in 'Step 2' would be best allocated to you.

STEP 4: IDENTIFY TASKS FOR OTHERS

Based on your strengths and weaknesses (step 1), identify what tasks in 'Step 2' would be best allocated to others.

STEP 5: IDENTIFY POSSIBLE TEAM MEMBERS

Can you think of people who may have skills that would match the tasks listed in 'step 2'? Write down the names of those people next to the appropriate task in 'step 2'.

STEP 5: CREATING A SHORT LIST

Review all the people you have listed next to tasks in 'step 2'. You now need to decide whether or not you want to share your goal with them. Can you see yourself working well with those people for the duration of your chosen goal? Could everyone that you have chosen, have the potential to work well together?

If the people listed have the skills and you would like to work with them, that leaves one thing to do. Time for you to connect with these people and check for their availability and enthusiasm to be a part of this adventure. Good luck in creating the perfect support team for your next adventure.

8. PRE-EVENT FULL DRESS REHEARSALS
Full dress rehearsals played a huge part in ensuring that I was ready on race day. These rehearsals also helped me develop my confidence.

The earlier dress rehearsals, broke me in every way possible and reduced me to tears. My weaknesses were highlighted ever so clearly, leaving me feeling defeated very early on in this adventure.

"Failure is a dress rehearsal for success." ~ Unknown

With each rehearsal, I found my weaknesses being replaced by a growing confidence. By the time I had completed my final dress rehearsal, I was feeling quietly confident.

When it was time to race, it was all about enjoying the moment. The hard work had been done and I had developed a belief that I could complete the 111km race. My support team had gone above and beyond with their tasks, which further fuelled my confidence.

Reflecting on my twelve months, I wonder what the race would have been like, if I hadn't put myself under pressure with a number of full dress rehearsals.

I feel as though the result could have been very different. The dress rehearsals provided with me a steep learning curve, which led to countless modifications.

Admittedly, I didn't enjoy the earlier dress rehearsals. It was certainly a relief to notice that each dress rehearsal indicated significant growth in all areas of my preparations.

Take the time now to consider how you can work some full dress rehearsals into your plan. Schedule dates into your timeline. Strategically place them to enable you to be at your best by the time your event comes around. Consider how many rehearsals would suit you.

9. IMMERSION

One of the best ways I have found to introduce habits or overcome fears, is through immersion. Immersion also proves to be a great way to develop skills and gain momentum.

I've used the immersion technique often with my karate training and decided that I would apply it to my paddling adventure.

As elegant as my paddle, capsize, swim routine may have looked from the outside, it wasn't the most efficient way to paddle 111km. I felt within myself, I needed to put some runs on the board and the immersion technique has always served me well.

As mentioned back in chapter two, my three month immersion included thirty minutes per day for three consecutive months. I wasn't always paddling. Sometimes, I would just go and sit in a kayak on the waters edge.

This immersion proved to be highly beneficial. I made considerable progress and my confidence was emerging in the paddling environment. The momentum I gained from this immersion, served me well all the way through to my Japan trip.

Take the time to review your goal and consider ways that you could give yourself a period of immersion. This period of immersion may help with refocusing, building momentum or growing your confidence.

You may even want to include more than one immersion on the way to achieving your goal. Immersions don't need to be three months in length. You can choose the length of your immersion based on your needs.

One final thought. Consider your current commitments and events that may conflict with your immersion period. Ask your support team for help if required, to enable you to complete your period of immersion.

"I am neither clever nor especially gifted. I am only very, very curious." ~ Albert Einstein

10, MEASURING PROGRESS

Hopefully by this point, you have your 'goal setting basics' in place and you have developed your plan with the previous nine elements.

On the road to achieving your goals, it is important that you have a variety of ways to assess your progress. You aren't always going to have somebody acknowledge your commitment and effort. And, you aren't always going to receive a trophy, medal or certificate to recognise your achievements and progress.

When I first started paddling, I bought a fancy watch which recorded data of each paddling session. I could view this data whilst I paddled, and I could go online after my session to study the data.

I measured things like distance, elapsed time, speed, average speed, heart rate and cadence. This watch even had a built in training partner. This was the perfect little toy to help with measuring my progress.

"I may not be there yet, but I'm closer than I was yesterday."
~ Unknown

I also liked to measure my progress by participating in a monthly private lesson with a local paddling coach, Peter Petho. Having Peter assessing me each month was great for my technique correction. My goal was to become a more efficient paddler before my big race.

Having myself filmed every so often was a great way to see myself in action. Peter would film me and share videos. Martin would also film me from time to time so I could assess my technique.

Working with the elements in The Beginner Blueprint also proved to be a great way for me to measure my progress. There was a great deal of testing and measuring with this adventure.

The pressure environment of the full dress rehearsals gave me a significant amount of feedback. But, I would have to say, that whether it be karate, paddling or life in general, my 'life basics' are my number one method of measuring my progress.

Consider ways in which you can measure your progress on the way to achieving your goals. The process of testing and measuring regularly, could make all the difference in how soon you achieve your goals.

Leading By Example

The Beginner Blueprint can apply to all areas of your life. It is also a great tool which can be shared with children more easily than you may realise. All that is required, is for you to 'lead by example'. Your actions speak louder than any words that you may speak.

"Parents must lead by example. Don't use the cliche; do as I say and not as I do. We are our children's first and most important role models."
~ Lee Haney

It is up to us as parents, caregivers and teachers to be open to learn about ourselves. The more we learn, the more we can grow. The more we grow, the more of a positive impact we may have on others.

As parents, caregivers and teachers, we are being observed at all times. Whether we like it or not, our habits are being modelled without us even realising. When you take a look at the special people in your life, you'll soon start to see a reflection of yourself. Do you like what you see, feel and hear?

I have an ever growing appreciation of the people in my life. I often feel as though I receive more than I give. Observing people in my life, gives me greater clarity. When I take the time to observe and learn,

I am guided to life changing thoughts which help me become a better version of myself.

When I think of what I would like to leave my children and students in my absence, there is not one material possession that comes to mind. What comes to mind is helping them:

- Develop themselves from the inside out.
- Help them to strengthen, expand and identify their personal power and realise their unique gifts.
- Respect, help and appreciate others.
- Develop as leaders. Do all they can to contribute to the uniting of families and communities.

The Beginner Blueprint will encourage growth within you from the inside out. You won't always be comfortable, but you will always be growing. Just remember that:

- freedom is on the other side of fear, so keep moving forward no matter how small the step.
- your time and effort to grow yourself now, may be the very thing that ensures that you, your children and students survive and thrive in this world.

Story: Inspirational People

ALL INTERACTIONS BEGIN AND END WITH RESPECT

A Breathe of Fresh Air

When this young boy entered our karate school, he had me puzzled for a moment. He was 'extremely' polite and respectful and a breathe of fresh air. I get to work with a lot of respectful kids, and I am very grateful, but Troy had clearly developed the habit of respect in his life.

Every day that Troy entered the dojo, I was greeted with a smile. He is always looking for ways to be of help and is a great helper when we are welcoming new students.

Troy is of primary school age and his parents must be extremely proud. I've had the pleasure of working with Troy for a couple of years now and he continues to come and thank me after every lesson.

Having Troy a part of our karate school reminds me daily of the importance of respect in our lives. No matter what we may be going through personally, we always have the ability to be respectful.

In the dojo, we are taught that karate begins and ends with respect. I've taken this one step further in my life. 'Life begins and ends with respect.'

MUSCLES FOR LIFE

RESPECT FOR OTHERS

Allow respect to be of primary importance when you interact with others. You don't always have to agree with others, but you can choose to deliver your words and actions in a respectful way.

We are all going to make mistakes. That is a part of the learning process. Accept that you are a work in progress and keep moving forward in a respectful way.

Consider what respect means to you, and choose a couple of things that you could do to demonstrate respect in your life. In your own time and in your own way, introduce these ideas into your life.

RESPECT FOR SELF

Most people I have spoken to, find it easier to be respectful to others, yet have found it difficult to be respectful to themselves.

Often we'll go throughout our day pleasing everyone else and forget about giving time to ourselves.

I mentioned 'life basics' on more than one occasion within The Beginner Blueprint, as it is a rock in my life. Choosing to develop my life basics, is a way which has helped me develop respect for myself.

Chapter 5

SHARE YOUR STORY

- Thank You For Reading The Beginner Blueprint
- Everybody Has A Story
- How To Submit Your Story

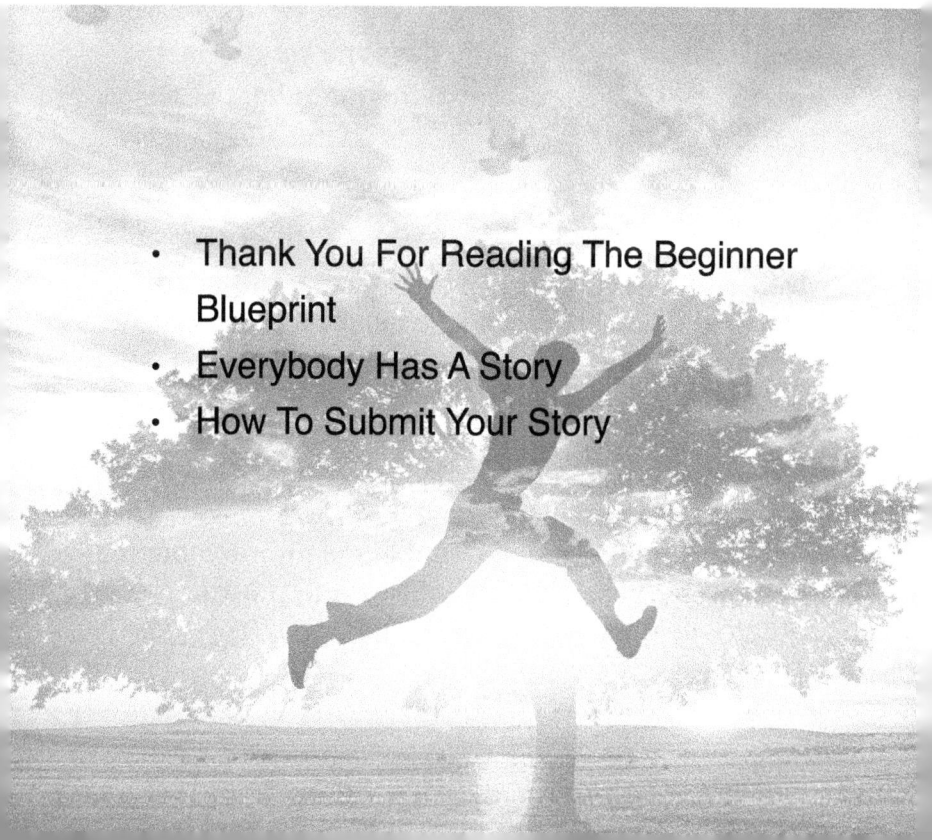

Thank you For Reading The Beginner Blueprint

Firstly, thank you for picking up and reading The Beginner Blueprint. The Beginner Blueprint is a powerful formula which I continue to use in my life. I'm currently using this same formula to help me publish my first books.

If you are reading this book, then you have proof that I survived. I'm proud to say that I have once again moved from 'Zero to Hero' in my husband's eyes. Even if it did take a few years to confront my fears with this challenge.

"You gave me your time, the most thoughtful gift of all."
~ Dan Zadra

There are great rewards when you share your story with others. I've always been reluctant to share my story, as I didn't think that it was anything special nor of any great value to anybody else. I am finding the opposite to be true.

On a personal level, this writing experience has taken a life changing experience and turned it into a powerful force in my life. It strengthens my very foundations with every piece of writing and propels me to greater heights.

It has given me the courage to step up and take on challenges. Challenges which I had already tagged unachieveable for me.

Prior to embracing and understanding The Beginner Blueprint, I felt as though I was in a glass box at times. Although I could see that a greater and more abundant world existed, I would often feel trapped. I doubted my abilities to bring my goals to life.

Since documenting 'The Beginner Blueprint' and 'Design Your Life And Enjoy Purposeful Living', the glass box that kept me from living my dreams, is no longer a barrier in my life. In fact, the act of sharing those documents, has all but shattered my glass box into little pieces.

More than anything, I would love to help others experience this same growth and sense of freedom. If you have ever felt as though you have been trapped and not able to break through, 'The Beginner Blueprint 'and 'Design Your Life And Enjoy Purposeful Living', may help you.

To further help you, I would like to encourage you to share your story with others. Everybody has a story and I would love to learn about your story.

Everybody Has a Story

W e all have a story. You have a unique story to share and I, personally, would like to learn from you. The act of reflecting, writing and sharing may help you see the value of your experiences.

We all have experiences. Every experience that you come across in your day is uniquely designed for you. There is a lesson attached to every experience. A lesson which will help you grow and enable you to achieve your goals at the most perfect time for you.

> "Everybody has a story to tell, a lesson to teach, and wisdom to share... Life is a beautiful masterpiece bound together by your experiences. Open up and share your story."
> ~ Melanie Koulouris

We are all here to help others. When you help others you may feel a sense of being valued. That feeling of being valued helps you stand a little taller and breathe a little deeper. Life can feel quite satisfying no matter what circumstances and events you may be facing.

We all have the ability to inspire others. When you are truly being yourself and embracing your life, you will naturally inspire others. Many of us spend much of our time trying to fit in and be like another person who appears to be popular.

You are different. You are meant to be different. It is these differences that make you special, unique and an inspiration to others. Learn about yourself and your gifts.

Deliberately use your gifts each day. Nurture and develop your gifts and allow yourself to shine in this world. The world doesn't need one kind of person. The world needs many kinds of people. People who accept, love and respect themselves. People who are willing to step up and share their gifts to help others.

As you are ready, please share your story. In sharing your story you become a light in this world which lights the path for others. We all need a little inspiration to help us move through our challenges. You don't know who is going to pick up and read your story and you don't know how many lives you will save.

The act of reflecting and writing about your story will have the greatest impact on your life; even if you were never to share with another person. The act of continual reflection and writing will guide you in the most perfect way to help you become the best version of yourself. And you never know, it may just save your life.

How To Submit Your Story

I would now like to invite you to share your story. In The Beginner Blueprint, I have shared my personal experiences and also shared stories of a few inspirational people. I have also shared more stories in, 'Design Your Life and Enjoy Purposeful Living'.

In my mind, the only thing missing is your story. I may never meet you, but I would love to learn more about your story.

"When you stand and share your story in an empowering way, your story will heal you and your story will heal somebody else."
~ Iyanla Vanzant

I will also be looking for stories to feature in upcoming books and on my website, so please note whether or not you would like your story featured. If you would like to remain anonymous please suggest an alias name that can be used.

I have set up a website which you can visit to submit your story. Please visit www.awayofliving.com.au

I look forward to learning more about you and being inspired by your story.

Chapter 6

ABOUT THE AUTHOR

Sandra Phillips

Sandra has been studying Chito-Ryu Karate-Do since 1990 and started her competitive career in 1993. Sandra has represented Australia on a number of occasions, competing at the International Chi-to-Ryu Karate-Do Championships since 1995, which is the highest level of competition for the style of Chi-to-Ryu Karate-Do.

Throughout her international competitive career, Sandra has consistently ranked in the top three in her division and winning gold in 2004.

Sandra's latest achievement was silver in 2013. Sandra has also helped husband Martin to coach students to achieve podium positions. Most recently four gold medalists in 2013.

In the year 2000, Sandra and husband Martin co-founded Sunshine Coast Karate in Maroochydore, Sunshine Coast, Australia.

Since the year 2000 they have worked with hundreds of people of all ages and not only in the dojo. They have also helped students transfer valuable life skills into their everyday lives. At the time of writing, Sandra and Martin were in the process of launching karate programs online.

SANDRA PHILLIPS

Sandra strives to grow with every day as a student of karate and of life, whilst actively documenting many valuable lessons along the way.

Sandra's greatest passion is, 'helping others'. In her words, *"there is no greater satisfaction than to help another person reach greater heights in their lives."*

> "Be the change you want to see in the world."
> ~ Mahatma Gandhi

After much encouragement, Sandra is now creating her 'A Way of Living' book series. 'The Beginner Blueprint' and 'Design Your Life And Enjoy Purposeful Living' are the first resources created for this series. Throughout 'A Way of Living' series, Sandra shares much of her learning with the goal to help people of all ages to:

- 'Survive' and 'thrive' in our rapidly changing world.
- Grow from the inside out. Strengthen, expand, identify personal power and realise unique gifts.
- Grow, respect and appreciate others. Become a person of service.
- Develop as leaders and contribute to the uniting of families and communities.

Do something today
that your future self
will say...

THANK YOU

A Way of Living Resources

DESIGN YOUR LIFE AND ENJOY
Purposeful Living

**HOLD ONTO YOUR DREAMS,
LET GO OF THE DETAILS
& ACT WITH LOVE**

THE BEGINNER
Blueprint

**FROM ZERO TO HERO, YOUR ROAD
MAP TO SUCCESS, NO MATTER
WHAT YOUR GOAL**

Please visit the website below to order 'A Way of Living' resources and to share your story.

www.aWayOfLiving.com.au

www.ingramcontent.com/pod-product-compliance
Lightning Source LLC
Chambersburg PA
CBHW071538040426
42452CB00008B/1055